ROSEMARY SHRAGER'S BAKES & CAKES & PUDDINGS

ROSEMARY SHRAGER'S BAKES & CAKES PUDDINGS

hamlyn

CONTENTS

INTRODUCTION

This is the third volume in my 'Absolutely Foolproof' series and I have to confess it is a book I never thought I would write. During my career as a chef, I didn't find pâtisserie particularly easy. It is a specialist area, one where you need to learn precise techniques, and I consider myself more of an instinctive cook. As a self-taught chef, I often had to learn on the job and, terrifyingly, was sometimes thrown in at the deep end. I managed to steer clear of the pastry section until I worked for Jean-Christophe Novelli in the late 1980s. He encouraged me to attempt fine pâtisserie for the first time and gave me a good grounding in the essential techniques. Later, I was lucky enough to spend two weeks on the pastry section at the Connaught Hotel in London – after I phoned up in despair because I was struggling to make croissants. Michel Bourdin, the legendary head chef, very kindly invited me in, and in no time at all I was handling the Rondo, a large machine for rolling and cutting pastry and croissant doughs. Working there was a fantastic experience and I emerged with a lovely croissant recipe, which I later honed in Ireland and at Bradford College – so I can safely say I have travelled far and wide in my search for the ultimate croissant (you'll find the recipe on page 56).

If I'm struggling with something, I like to go back to the source to find out what I should be doing. I hope you will be able to use this book as your source, to help you with all your baking queries. I have tried to include all the information you will need for success – the information that I found so hard to come by all those years ago.

Because I lacked confidence when I started out, I understand how nervous baking can make people feel. Being a good baker is a matter of learning a series of logical steps. Baking is as much a science as an art, and understanding why certain things happen is crucial. If you don't understand what you are trying to achieve, it can all go horribly wrong! I'm convinced that many people who think they are hopeless at baking have been deterred by one bad experience. So in this book there are plenty of tips that highlight the crucial stages in a recipe and guide you through them safely.

The book covers all the areas that are traditionally the responsibility of the pastry chef: that's everything from breads, pies, pastry, cakes and biscuits to ice creams, mousses, puddings, cordials and compotes. Even canapés and savoury pies are part of the pastry chef's remit. They require the same skills and techniques as sweet dishes, so there is a logic to including them. Some of the sections are more challenging than others – Danish pastries, for example, are clearly going to require more time and effort than sorbets. So the best thing to do is tackle the chapters in the order you feel comfortable with.

For the more complex recipes, always allow yourself plenty of time. The nice thing about making bread, pastry and cakes is that you can set aside an afternoon to tackle them and there is no pressure to get them on the table at a certain time, as there is when you are cooking dinner. The other thing to bear in mind is that lengthy recipes can usually be tackled in stages. Professional chefs prepare things in advance to make life easier, and it makes perfect sense to do this at home too. As long as they don't rely on whisked egg whites for their rise, most cake mixtures can be made several hours before you need them and kept in the fridge until you are ready to bake. Even for something as simple as fairy cakes, it can be good to get ahead with making the batter. Pastry can be prepared the day before and left in the fridge, and so can bread doughs, ice cream bases and Italian meringue, which is used as a topping for tarts and puddings or as a base for mousses.

At the other end of the scale, if you want something in a hurry, you will find plenty in this book that will fit the bill: a quick soda loaf for when you've run out of bread, a simple dish of poached fruit to celebrate the best of summer's produce or a syllabub that can be whipped up in minutes from storecupboard ingredients.

Some of the recipes in this book are not the kind of thing that people regularly make at home, but I would love it if they were. Baking is the ideal leisure activity and it's wonderful when you can take the time to do something from scratch. I love the idea of making all the elements of a black forest gateau, for example, or baking your own Danish pastries or profiteroles. It goes without saying that they will taste infinitely better than the ones you can buy.

Looking through the recipes, they fall mainly into two categories: classic French pâtisserie and traditional British cooking. Although I have always worked in the classic French style, I was brought up in the great British tradition of steamed puddings and comfort food, and both strands are very dear to my heart. I truly believe that a steamed pudding can be every bit as sophisticated as a fruit bavarois. There was a time when French cooking was taken more seriously than our native dishes, but now, thank goodness, we can celebrate them both and accept that a British trifle should take its place next to a classic French apple tart in the canon of great desserts.

Making desserts and baked goods can be one of life's simple pleasures. I hope this book will give you the confidence to tackle something new, whether it's making perfect pastry, baking delectable cakes and breads or creating beautiful ice creams and sorbets. The vast majority of the recipes are ones I have been using successfully for many years and I shall be thrilled if they bring you as much pleasure as they have given me.

NOTES ON THE RECIPES

- All spoon measures are level unless otherwise stated.

- All eggs are large unless otherwise stated. I much prefer to use good free-range eggs for the best colour and flavour.

- I recommend fine sea salt for bread making. Otherwise, I use ordinary flaky sea salt.

- Pepper should always be freshly ground. I use white pepper when I don't want to see the black grains in a dish, but I do use black whenever I can, as I prefer the flavour.

- I favour unsalted butter, as I like to add my own salt to a recipe and I find I can control the flavour better in this way.

- I use organic flour from the Sunflours mill, near Ripon in North Yorkshire. I recommend you seek out a good local flour if possible, as it makes all the difference to your baking.

- It is very important to buy a good set of knives. For me, they are the tools of my trade. I use Wüsthof knives, as they handle well and have a good weight.

- A surprisingly useful piece of kitchen equipment is a flexible paint scraper. I bought one 35 years ago and use it like a palette knife. I call it my swish, and if I lost it I would probably have to give up work.

CONVERSION CHARTS

OVEN TEMPERATURES

°C	°C (fan)	°F	Gas Mark
110°C	90°C	225°F	¼
120°C	100°C	250°F	½
140°C	120°C	275°F	1
150°C	130°C	300°F	2
160°C	140°C	325°F	3
180°C	160°C	350°F	4
190°C	170°C	375°F	5
200°C	180°C	400°F	6
220°C	200°C	425°F	7
230°C	210°C	450°F	8
240°C	220°C	475°F	9

SPOONS

1 teaspoon = one 5ml spoon
1 tablespoon = one 15ml spoon

WEIGHTS

5g	¼oz
15g	½oz
20g	¾oz
25g	1oz
50g	2oz
75g	3oz
125g	4oz
150g	5oz
175g	6oz
200g	7oz
250g	8oz
275g	9oz
300g	10oz
325g	11oz
375g	12oz
400g	13oz
425g	14oz
475g	15oz
500g	1lb
625g	1¼lb
750g	1½lb
875g	1¾lb
1kg	2lb
1.25kg	2½lb
1.5kg	3lb
1.75kg	3½lb
2kg	4lb

VOLUME

15ml	½ fl oz
25ml	1 fl oz
50ml	2 fl oz
75ml	3 fl oz
100ml	3½ fl oz
125ml	4 fl oz
150ml	¼ pint
175ml	6 fl oz
200ml	7 fl oz
250ml	8 fl oz
275ml	9 fl oz
300ml	½ pint
325ml	11 fl oz
350ml	12 fl oz
375ml	13 fl oz
400ml	14 fl oz
450ml	¾ pint
475ml	16 fl oz
500ml	17 fl oz
575ml	18 fl oz
600ml	1 pint
750ml	1¼ pints
900ml	1½ pints
1 litre	1¾ pints
1.2 litres	2 pints
1.5 litres	2½ pints
1.8 litres	3 pints
2 litres	3½ pints
2.5 litres	4 pints

MEASUREMENTS

2.5mm	⅛ inch
5mm	¼ inch
1cm	½ inch
2cm	¾ inch
2.5cm	1 inch
5cm	2 inches
7cm	3 inches
10cm	4 inches
12cm	5 inches
15cm	6 inches
18cm	7 inches
20cm	8 inches
23cm	9 inches
25cm	10 inches
28cm	11 inches
30cm	12 inches

BAKING BASICS

When I visit a kitchenware department I'm like a kid in a sweet shop. I get so excited when I see all the different-shaped tins and I love specialist items such as jelly moulds, shortbread tins and biscuit cutters. The choice nowadays is better than it's ever been, and it's so easy to get carried away. As far as ingredients are concerned, you can get pretty much everything you need from a supermarket, but it's fun to jolly up your storecupboard with baking ingredients from specialist shops. Most of them will keep for ages and can be used to add interest to cakes and puddings.

EQUIPMENT

TINS AND BAKING SHEETS

Baking sheets need to be heavy duty so that they don't buckle in the heat of the oven. Buy a good one and it will last a lifetime. It's also worth investing in a really top-quality, deep, heavy-based pan for pâtisserie work such as making caramel – you risk it burning if you use a thin, cheap pan.

I like to use flexible silicone moulds for small things such as petits fours, and also find them incredibly useful for frozen desserts such as parfaits because they are so easy to peel off. However, I am yet to be convinced that they are better for large cakes and loaves. For cakes, I find springform tins are best – again, because they are so easy to remove. Straight-sided loaf tins with distinct corners make really handsome loaves, and have the advantage that you can use them for making terrines too.

When making tarts, I've always preferred a metal ring set on a baking sheet rather than a tart tin, for the sheer ease of removing the ring after baking. If you decide to go for tins instead, be sure to choose loose-bottomed ones. Traditional double-crust pies are best baked in a shallow metal pie plate.

A selection of little moulds is always useful, with dariole moulds being perhaps the most useful of all. They are ideal for panna cotta, crème caramel, sponge puddings, jellies, mousses and custards. Always buy non-stick ones and, if you are worried about turning out the contents, brush the moulds with a little flavourless oil before use.

BOWLS AND DISHES

My feeling with mixing bowls is the bigger the better. It's always easier if you have more space, particularly when folding mixtures together. You can buy bowls with rubber bases, which stops them slipping.

For steamed puddings, traditional china pudding basins are great. They come in a wide range of sizes, are very hardwearing and not expensive. Gratin dishes also come in a variety of sizes, but I like to use slightly deeper ones rather than the very shallow dishes.

I absolutely love old-fashioned jelly moulds. In the Victorian era, they were such a novelty and I do believe it is time they became fashionable again.

MACHINES

You can get by without any expensive machines at all if needs be, and do all your beating, whipping, chopping and mixing by hand. But owning the correct equipment does cut down on labour and makes life so much easier. It really opens up what you can achieve at home.

If you are on a tight budget, the best investment is a handheld electric beater, which will cope well with beating and whisking. Sometimes they have dough hooks too. For some tasks, though, such as making Italian meringue, a freestanding electric mixer is invaluable. The KitchenAid is my current favourite and performs really well.

Once you have a food processor, you will wonder how you ever managed without it – it makes short work of purées and can also be used for pastry. An ice cream maker is arguably not an essential but is a great thing to ask for as a present.

STIRRING, WHISKING ETC

Despite being very fond of my KitchenAid, I still favour balloon whisks for whisking egg whites because they are easy to control and give great volume. They are also useful for general mixing and for smoothing out sauces.

Swiss roll tin

Baking sheet

Madeleine tin

Baking mat

Sandwich tins

Springform cake tins

Loaf tins

Dariole moulds

Wire racks

Baking parchment

Tart tins

Ice cream maker

Freestanding electric mixer

Blowtorch

Dough scraper

Piping bag and nozzles

Handheld electric beater

Food processor

I love using big spatulas because they are easier to work with than small ones. The all-in-one, heat-resistant spatulas are brilliant – and you can use them in non-stick pans.

One of my indispensable kitchen tools is a cranked, or stepped, palette knife. It makes short work of smoothing icing on cakes and levelling cake batters in the tin before baking.

A selection of wooden spoons are, of course, essential in any kitchen. Metal spoons are best for folding because they cut through the mixture. It's also worth making sure you have a large slotted spoon for draining poached fruit.

KNIVES

Even when baking, you still need a decent selection of knives. A cook's knife for chopping and a paring knife with a slightly curved blade are useful for fruit. A zester or a Microplane is essential for removing the zest from citrus fruit. A U-shaped vegetable peeler is just as handy for peeling apples and pears as it is for vegetables.

OTHER USEFUL ITEMS

For pastry, it's essential to have a good, solid rolling pin. The ones without handles are best. They are usually wider, so you can roll out a larger piece of pastry and it's easier to apply even pressure. You will also need a large pastry brush, about 22cm long, for brushing flour off puff pastry, and smaller brushes for glazing. I find the traditional ones much easier to use than the silicone versions.

I do love my silicone baking mats, though. They last forever and they are machine washable. Having two in your kitchen just makes life so much easier. You can bake meringues, tuiles, biscuits, savoury pastries, bread etc. on them.

For piping, I like to use disposable bags. They're not very expensive and it simply seems more hygienic. You can cut the end to fit your piping nozzle. Also, it's very useful to be able to leave a full piping bag in the fridge.

Finally, a good fine conical, or chinois, sieve is invaluable. It's much easing for straining puréed fruit because you can just push it through with a ladle.

STORECUPBOARD INGREDIENTS

FLOURS AND GRAINS

Flour and grains keep well, but it's worth checking the dates regularly because they can turn rancid. You can also occasionally get tiny mites in your flour. Keeping it in a sealed container helps guard against this. If you have a good wholefood shop nearby, it's worth buying flour there, as they usually sell interesting ones, often stoneground, and you might be able to get a locally milled flour.

Strong flour is made from hard varieties of wheat and is therefore higher in gluten, which makes it most suitable for bread making. Rye flour is lower in gluten and therefore makes quite a heavy loaf that is slow to rise. It is best used in combination with other flours when making bread – I prefer it with white. You really don't need a lot of rye flour in a loaf, but it does improve the flavour. Wholemeal flour has all the nutrients of the grain left in it and also gives a wonderfully well-flavoured loaf.

Plain white flour has had all the wheatgerm removed and has usually been bleached. The very best is stoneground and unbleached, giving it a creamier colour. Self-raising flour has had raising agents added. If you don't have any, you can add baking powder to plain flour – usually in the ratio of 25g to 450g (check the baking powder tub; they often recommend how much to use for various types of baking).

Oatmeal is made from oats that have been milled to a coarse, medium or fine texture – or the even coarser pinhead, which I love. Oatmeal and rolled oats are perfect for wholesome baking – think oaty biscuits, flapjacks and oatcakes. They can also be added to cakes and crumble toppings.

Cornflour, a starch made from maize, is most often used for thickening sauces and custards. It can be added to shortbread or pastry for a firmer texture – although if you add a little to meringues it has the opposite effect, making them softer, as in the classic Pavlova. Polenta is another form of maize. It gives its lovely golden colour and rough texture to breads, cakes and pastries.

SUGARS AND SWEETENERS

Granulated sugar is cheaper than caster and is ideal if you are using it in a recipe where the sugar needs to dissolve, such as syrups. I tend to use granulated sugar when making caramel and cooking fruits. Caster sugar is useful for absolutely everything and is the one to go for in cake mixtures that are creamed together. Golden caster is a more natural sugar and is a lovely product to work with.

Golden syrup is best used in melted mixtures such as gingerbreads, flapjacks and some biscuits. Black treacle has a very distinctive taste and is often used in combination with golden syrup to give a milder result. Clear honey is generally easier to use in baking than set honey – though sometimes the flavour of set honey is better. Liquid glucose is worth buying if you are making sorbets and ice creams, as it helps give them a really smooth texture.

Icing sugar is, of course, used for making icings and for dusting cakes and desserts. It's also the best way to sweeten fruit purées that don't require cooking, as it dissolves without heat. You can now get a wonderful golden icing sugar that has a slightly honeyed colour and a delicious flavour. Brown sugars also have a distinctive flavour, almost toffeeish in the case of the darker ones. I love to use them in fruit cakes, Christmas pudding, nut tarts – anywhere you need richness as well as sweetness. They can become rock hard once opened, so do keep them tightly sealed. I have heard that giving them a few seconds in the microwave can soften them.

DRIED FRUIT

Dried fruit should be kept very well wrapped because it can become dried out and stale. Raisins, sultanas and particularly currants have to be checked thoroughly for stalks before use. I always wash them as well. I like to use seedless raisins, and the large muscat ones are especially delicious. Soft, ready-to-eat apricots and figs are best for baking, but for stewing you can use the harder ones and let them plump up in the liquid.

Candied peel is available ready chopped but the flavour is so much fresher if you buy large pieces and cut them up yourself. For glacé cherries, look for the darker, undyed ones rather than the bright red ones.

Stem ginger in syrup is really useful. It's effectively two ingredients in one – the ginger itself and the syrup, which you can use to flavour all kinds of puddings. I also like crystallised ginger, which you can chop finely and add to cakes.

NUTS AND SEEDS

Most nuts can be bought whole or ready chopped. Because they are rich in oil, they go off quite quickly, so buy small quantities and be sure to use them well within their best-before date.

Nuts can be roasted in the oven or a dry frying pan to improve their flavour. Almonds are arguably the most useful – you can buy them whole, blanched, flaked, nibbed and ground. Ground almonds – and hazelnuts – make the most delicious moist cakes with great keeping qualities.

Like nuts, seeds can become stale quickly because of the oils they contain. They are lovely to have in your cupboard, however, and should be used wherever possible, as they are little powerhouses of nutrition. They are fantastic sprinkled on breads and added to biscuits and flapjacks. Caraway seeds are not to everyone's taste, but I love them in breads and cakes. Poppy seeds make the most delicious

cakes and are brilliant scattered on bread rolls and plaits after glazing.

SPICES

Ground spices should be bought in small quantities so that you don't keep them too long. Whole spices, ground as you need them, always have a fresher flavour. Do buy whole nutmeg and invest in a little nutmeg grater – the flavour is incomparable.

Saffron is one of my favourite spices, for both colour and flavour. Be sure to buy the real thing – i.e. saffron strands. They have a reputation for being expensive, but you need only a little at a time.

Vanilla pods should be plump and soft – if you see hard sticks, avoid them, as it means they have been around for far too long. It's really worth paying a bit extra for decent vanilla pods. You can also buy pots of vanilla seed paste, which makes a good alternative. Vanilla extract gives a good flavour, but do not buy synthetic essence – it isn't a patch on the real thing.

OTHER USEFUL INGREDIENTS

Other useful storecupboard ingredients include baking powder and/or cream of tartar and bicarbonate of soda. Baking powder is essentially two parts cream of tartar to one part bicarbonate of soda, so you can always make up your own.

Gelatine keeps really well and is worth having in stock. The leaves give better results than the powder and are actually easier to use. If you are vegetarian, agar agar makes a good substitute for gelatine in most instances.

Chocolate is great to have in for impromptu cakes and desserts – though it requires a certain amount of willpower! It's best kept at cool room temperature rather than in the fridge.

I like to use fresh yeast but, for emergencies, keep a packet of active dried yeast in your cupboard.

TECHNIQUES

WHISKING

Although you can whisk with an electric mixer, I much prefer to use a balloon whisk, as it gives more volume. Whisking by hand can be tiring, but try to keep your wrist loose and then it will be easier. Keep the bowl tilted slightly while whisking, so that the mixture goes to one side and you get more depth.

If you are whisking egg whites on their own, it's always better to whisk them to soft rather than stiff peaks, as they can split easily. However, if you are whisking them with sugar, the sugar will stabilise and bind them. This means you can whisk for much longer without the egg whites splitting, and take them to stiff peaks. Do whisk the whites to soft peaks before adding the sugar, though, otherwise they won't stiffen up.

To check which stage the whites have reached, lift up the whisk with some of the beaten egg white on it: soft peaks will flop over slightly, while stiff peaks will be completely upright. When the whites are whisked to firm peaks, you should be able to turn the bowl upside down over your head and they won't move.

When you're whisking double cream, it's best to under-whip it slightly if you will be adding it to another mixture – for example, when making a mousse. The cream will continue to thicken slightly as you fold it in.

FOLDING

Folding is a technique used to retain air in a mixture when combining ingredients – for example, when adding flour to cake mixtures or cream to mousses. Traditionally a large metal spoon is recommended for folding, but I like to use a large, thin spatula. Never fold with a wooden spoon – it is too thick and will knock the air out.

When you fold two mixtures together, take the edge of your spatula around the edge of the bowl and bring it back up so that the mixture turns over. Remember to take it through the middle of the mixture too; some people do a figure of eight. As you fold, turn the bowl in the opposite direction with your other hand – this speeds up the process and helps you fold everything together more efficiently.

ROLLING

Rolling out pastry is quite personal and everyone develops their own style to some extent. In my experience, many people find it difficult to roll out a neat rectangle or circle. All you need to do is place your ball of pastry on the work surface, press it down lightly with the palm of your hand to flatten it a little, then roll it out with a rolling pin, stopping just short of the edge of the pastry. The trick is to make sure you dust the work surface lightly with flour, plus a scant dusting on top of the pastry, so that the rolling pin doesn't stick. Gently put your hand underneath and turn it 45 degrees every few rolls. This should give you a perfect circle. However, most people roll more strongly on one side than the other, so check the thickness of the pastry regularly to make sure it is even.

When the pastry reaches a certain size, you will need to roll it up loosely over the rolling pin to move it, supporting it with your other hand, then unroll the pastry again.

LINING

The methods for preparing and lining depend on the size and shape of your tin. Opposite are step-by-step instructions for how to line four of the most commonly used baking tins.

How to line the base of a round tin

1 Take a square of baking parchment a few centimetres larger than your cake tin. Fold 2 opposite corners together to make a triangle.

2 Keep folding it in half until you have a long, thin triangle. Turn the cake tin upside down and place the small point of the triangle in the centre.

3 Trim off the part of the triangle that overlaps the edge of the tin. Unfold the triangle and you have a circle that fits the base of the tin. Grease the tin and place the circle in it.

How to line the base and sides of a round tin

1 Line the base of the tin as described above. Measure the length and height of the side of the tin.

2 Cut a long strip of baking parchment to fit.

3 Put the strip of parchment into the greased tin, making sure it adheres to the side.

How to line a loaf tin

1 Cut a strip of parchment long enough to cover the base and the short sides of the tin, allowing for a 2cm overlap at each side.

2 Position the paper in the greased tin.

3 Make sure it fits the short edges neatly. The overlapping parchment is useful for removing the cake from the tin.

How to line a square tin

1 Cut a square of baking parchment large enough to cover the base and sides. Fold the part of the paper that will cover each side of the tin over.

2 Straighten the folded sides so that they stand up. Using scissors, cut down diagonally at each corner to the point where the 2 folds intersect.

3 Place the baking parchment in the greased tin, fitting it into the corners – you can staple the corner flaps together if you like.

BREADS

Bread is not difficult to make and neither will it take up much of your time — just half an hour or so for mixing and kneading the dough, then a few minutes after it has risen to knock it back and shape it. While it is rising, you can be getting on with something else entirely. If you make soda bread, such as the Wheaten Soda Bread on page 44, all you need to do is mix it and put it in the oven, since it doesn't rely on yeast to help it rise. Commercial bread is proved very rapidly and has various enzymes added, which many people find difficult to digest. Making bread at home means you can let it rise slowly — so much better for you, and the flavour will be better too.

The traditional way to make a sourdough loaf is with a yeast-free starter, which creates its own fermentation. You have to 'feed' it by adding flour to it each day. This recipe uses a foolproof starter that contains a little yeast to keep it stable and doesn't need feeding. If you love sourdough and don't want the hassle of looking after a starter, this is the way to do it.

LIGHT SOURDOUGH BREAD

To make the basic Sourdough Starter, follow steps 1 to 4
To tear, roll and turn the dough, follow steps 9 to 12
To knock back the dough, follow step 16

MAKES 1 MEDIUM LOAF

150g rye flour

300g plain flour, plus extra for dusting

14g fresh yeast

150ml lukewarm water

8g fine sea salt

FOR THE SOURDOUGH STARTER:

6g fresh yeast

250ml lukewarm water

150g plain flour

1 To make the starter, crumble the yeast into a bowl, then whisk with the water.

2 Gradually add the flour, whisking all the time.

3 Cover and leave to stand for 1–2 days in the fridge or a cool place, or 24 hours at room temperature (around 20°C).

4 The mixture will develop bubbles on the surface and acquire a sour smell.

5 When the starter is ready, put the 2 flours into a large mixing bowl.

6 Crumble in the yeast and mix well.

7 Add the starter, pour in the water and mix well to form a dough.

8 Lightly flour the work surface.

9 Hold the dough at the nearest edge with the fingers of one hand and push the rest of it away with the heel of your other hand to tear the dough.

10 Roll the dough back on itself and give it a quarter turn.

11 Then repeat the tearing, rolling and turning for about 10 minutes, until it begins to feel elastic.

12 Your hands will become sticky, so dip them regularly into a bowl of flour, clapping your hands together to shake off the excess.

13 Sprinkle the salt over the dough.

14 Continue the tearing, rolling and turning for another 5 minutes.

15 Place the dough in a floured bowl, cover with cling film and allow to rise at room temperature for 1 hour, until doubled in size.

16 Knock back the dough by gently hitting it to knock out the air.

17 Briefly tear, roll and turn, then shape into a circle and place on a floured baking sheet.

18 Using a sharp knife, make a cross on top, then set aside to rise at room temperature for 30–40 minutes.

19 Bake in an oven preheated to 190°C/Gas Mark 5 for 30 minutes. Then remove the loaf from the oven.

20 Tap the bottom with your knuckles; if it sounds hollow, it is done. If not, put it back in the oven upside down for about 10 minutes.

21 Place the loaf on a wire rack to cool.

sourdough variation

Dense Sourdough Bread – make the starter as on page 23, steps 1–4. When it's ready, put 300g rye flour and 150g plain flour in a bowl. Crumble in 5g fresh yeast and mix well. Add the starter and 150ml water and mix again. Tear, roll and turn as described on pages 23–24, steps 9–14, adding 8g salt at the appropriate point. Follow steps 15–21 to complete the loaf.

Yeast-free Starter Dough – mix 25g rye flour and 40ml lukewarm water in a bowl, cover with cling film and leave at room temperature for 24 hours. (Ideally the temperature should be around 28°C, but don't worry if it's lower than that – it will just take a little longer to ferment. When ready it should look sloppy.) At that point, add another 25g rye flour and 40ml lukewarm water to the mixture, cover and set aside as before. Repeat this once more. On the fourth day follow the main recipe from step 5 on page 23. You might need to add a little extra water to achieve a soft, kneadable consistency.

TIPS AND IDEAS

■ The longer you leave the starter dough before use, the better the flavour. If possible, leave it for 3 days.

■ You can double the starter dough and store half of it in the fridge – it will keep for a couple of days, ready for your next loaf.

■ I like to use fresh yeast in all my bread, but if you prefer dried or easy-blend, use half the weight of the fresh yeast and add it according to the instructions on the packet.

■ Fresh yeast should be nice and crumbly, with a pleasant smell. Store it in the fridge and use within 2 weeks. Some people recommend freezing it, but I find that it loses some of its strength after freezing.

■ If the water is cold when you mix it with the flours, the dough will still rise – it will just take longer.

■ Rye flour is low in gluten, so it will take a while to come together into a smooth dough.

■ Salt retards the action of the yeast, so I prefer to mix it in towards the end of kneading, rather than adding it at the beginning with the other ingredients.

■ Do not be tempted to add flavourings to this dough – the rye flour and the starter provide all the flavour you need. However, you can sprinkle some seeds, such as poppy or sesame, on the top before baking, if you like.

■ Bread keeps better at room temperature than in the fridge. It does freeze very successfully, though, so it is worth doubling up the quantities here and storing one loaf in the freezer.

APULIAN BREAD

I was given this recipe a very long time ago. I love the idea of covering it with a bowl to prove, as this ensures it has a lovely smooth, domed top. The loaf is very light, yet holds together so well, and it toasts like a dream — fantastic served toasted and rubbed with garlicky olive oil.

Makes 2 loaves

1kg strong white flour, plus extra for dusting

15g fresh yeast

700ml lukewarm water

1 tablespoon fine sea salt

For the starter:

150g strong white flour

5g fresh yeast (1 packed ½ teaspoon)

100ml lukewarm water

olive oil for greasing

1 Make the starter the day before you want the loaf. Put the flour in a bowl, crumble in the yeast, then add the water and mix well. Transfer the dough to a bowl lightly greased with olive oil, cover tightly with cling film and place in a warm, draught-free place overnight. It should more than double in size.

2 The next day put the flour in a bowl, crumble in the yeast and mix in the starter, adding enough of the water to make a fairly stiff dough. On a lightly floured work surface, tear, roll and turn the dough for 10 minutes (see page 23, steps 9–11). Add the salt and continue the tearing, rolling and turning for another 5 minutes. Dust the bowl with flour, place the dough in it, then cover with cling film and leave at room temperature for about 1 hour, until the dough has doubled in size.

3 Carefully knock back the dough (see page 24, step 16) and turn it on to a floured work surface. Briefly tear, roll and turn it, then shape it into 2 round loaves. Place them on 2 floured baking sheets, cover each loaf with a large floured glass bowl that allows for expansion and leave to rise at room temperature for 45 minutes–1 hour, until doubled in size.

4 Remove the bowls, dust the loaves with flour and bake in an oven preheated to 220°C/Gas Mark 7 for 20 minutes. Lower the heat to 190°C/Gas Mark 5 and bake for another 30 minutes, or until the loaves sound hollow when tapped on the bottom. Place on a wire rack until completely cold.

TOMATO AND ANCHOVY RING

The trick with this impressive-looking bread is to make sure the filling is completely cold before you add it. It's a substantial loaf, great for picnics and very popular with children.

Makes 1 ring

600g strong white flour, plus extra for dusting

25g fresh yeast

400ml lukewarm water

fine sea salt

oil for greasing

For the filling:

1 small red onion, finely chopped

2 tablespoons olive oil

400g tomatoes, deseeded and diced

leaves from a sprig of thyme

12 white anchovy fillets in oil, drained and chopped

1 First make the filling. Soften the onion in the olive oil, add the tomatoes and thyme and cook gently for 20 minutes, until all the juices have evaporated. Add the anchovies, stirring until they disintegrate, then process the mixture in a food processor or blender to a paste. Set aside until completely cold.

2 Put the flour in a bowl, crumble in the yeast, then add enough of the water to make a firm dough. On a lightly floured work surface, tear, roll and turn the dough for 7 minutes (see page 23, steps 9–11), then add 1 teaspoon salt and continue tearing, rolling and turning for a further 5 minutes. Place in an oiled bowl, cover with cling film and leave to rise at room temperature for 1 hour, or until doubled in size.

3 Carefully knock back the dough (see page 24, step 16) and turn it on to a floured work surface. Roll it into a rectangle about 4mm thick. Spread the tomato mixture over the dough, leaving a 3cm border all round. Roll up lengthways, bring the ends together to form a ring and squeeze to seal. Place seam-side down on a floured baking sheet and leave to rise at room temperature for 1 hour, or until doubled in size.

4 Bake in an oven preheated to 200°C/Gas Mark 6 for 40–45 minutes, until it sounds hollow when tapped on the bottom. Cool on a wire rack or eat straight away.

FOUGASSE WITH LEMON AND GARLIC

This is a lovely bread to make, and great served with dips. Make sure you get the correct tear shape.

Makes 2 fougasses

325g strong white flour, plus extra for dusting

10g fresh yeast

about 225ml lukewarm water

1½ tablespoons olive oil, plus extra for sprinkling

7.5g fine sea salt

zest of 2 lemons, finely chopped

4 garlic cloves, chopped

1 Put the flour into a bowl, crumble in the fresh yeast and mix well. Add the water and oil and mix to form a dough, adding a little more water if it feels too dry.

2 Turn the dough on to a floured work surface and tear, roll and turn it for 10 minutes (see page 23, steps 9–11). Sprinkle with the salt and continue tearing, rolling and turning for a further 5 minutes, until smooth and elastic. Shape the dough into a ball, place in a lightly floured bowl, then cover loosely with cling film and leave to rise at room temperature for about 1 hour, until it has doubled in size.

3 Carefully knock back the dough (see page 24, step 16), add the lemon zest and garlic and gently work them in. Cut the dough in half. On a lightly floured work surface, roll each piece into an oval about 5mm thick. Using a sharp knife, cut 3 deep slits at an angle across the top of each loaf. Stretch each loaf slightly so that the slits open up a little and look like a ladder. Place each loaf on a floured baking sheet and leave to rise at room temperature for 30 minutes.

4 Sprinkle the loaves with olive oil, place in an oven preheated to 220°C/Gas Mark 7 and bake for 15–20 minutes, until golden brown. The bread is ready if it sounds hollow when tapped on the bottom. Place on a wire rack to cool.

THYME BREAD

I like to add a generous amount of thyme to this loaf. A mini food processor is useful for chopping it to a pulp, as this brings out the flavour. If you haven't got one, though, just chop it as finely as you can – it doesn't matter if it isn't quite a pulp.

Makes 2 loaves

600g strong white flour, plus extra for dusting

18g fresh yeast

400ml lukewarm water

8g fine sea salt

2 tablespoons thyme leaves, blended to a pulp

1 Put the flour in a bowl, crumble in the yeast, then add the water and mix to a soft dough. Place on a lightly floured work surface and tear, roll and turn it for 10 minutes (see page 23, steps 9–11). Add the salt and thyme and continue tearing, rolling and turning for a further 5 minutes, until the dough is elastic. Transfer to a floured bowl, cover with cling film and leave to rise at room temperature for about 1 hour, until doubled in size.

2 Carefully knock back the dough (see page 24, step 16), cut it in half and shape into 2 loaves about 22cm long. Place on 2 separate floured baking sheets and leave to rise again at room temperature for about 40 minutes.

3 Bake in an oven preheated to 220°C/Gas Mark 7 for 25 minutes, then lower the heat to 160°C/Gas Mark 3 and bake for another 20 minutes. The bread is ready if it sounds hollow when tapped on the bottom. Cool on a wire rack.

BAGELS

Bagels are unique for their traditional double cooking method. The initial boiling gives them a dense, firm texture, then they are baked until golden. I had my first bagel 40 years ago in the East End of London at 2 in the morning and I'll never forget it. It had just been baked and was served with smoked salmon — absolutely delicious.

Makes about 12

350ml lukewarm water

15g fresh yeast

500g strong white flour, plus extra for dusting

50g caster sugar

5g fine sea salt

oil for greasing

coarse sea salt or mixed seeds (e.g. caraway, poppy and sesame) for the topping

1 Put 100ml of the water in a small bowl and crumble in the yeast. Mix well, then leave for 15 minutes, until it becomes frothy.

2 Place the flour and sugar in a bowl, add the yeast mixture and the remaining water and mix well to form a dough.

3 Put the dough on a floured work surface and tear, roll and turn it for 10 minutes (see page 23, steps 9–11). Add the salt and continue tearing, rolling and turning for another 5 minutes. Place in a floured bowl, cover with cling film and leave to rise at room temperature for about 1 hour, until doubled in size.

4 Put a large pan of water on to boil, then reduce to a simmer. Meanwhile, carefully knock back the dough (see page 24, step 16) and cut into pieces, each weighing 75g. Roll into balls, then press a piping nozzle into the middle of each piece to make a hole. Stretch the holes with your fingers to make them about 4cm wide. Place the bagels on a large floured baking sheet.

5 Depending on the size of your pan, put 2 or 3 bagels at a time into the simmering water; do not overcrowd it. Cook for 1 minute, then carefully turn the bagels over and cook for another minute. Remove with a slotted spoon, drain well and place on an oiled baking sheet. Repeat with all the remaining bagels. Sprinkle with coarse sea salt or mixed seeds and bake in an oven preheated to 220°C/Gas Mark 7 for about 20 minutes. Set aside to cool on a wire rack before eating.

NAAN BREAD

This is such a fun thing to make – children love to help, and often welcome it in their packed lunches. You can add flavourings, if you like.

Makes 6

100ml milk

12g fresh yeast

300g plain white flour, plus extra for dusting

1 teaspoon baking powder

2 teaspoons caster sugar

50g crème fraîche

1 tablespoon corn oil or vegetable oil, plus extra for greasing or frying

1 teaspoon sea salt, plus any other flavourings you wish to add, e.g. mustard seeds or onion seeds

1 Heat the milk until just warm. Pour into a small bowl and crumble in the yeast. Stir twice, then leave for 15 minutes, until frothy.

2 Put the flour, baking powder and sugar into a bowl. Add the yeast mixture, crème fraîche and oil and bring together with your hands. Tear, roll and turn the dough for 5 minutes (see page 23, steps 9–11). Add the salt and any other flavouring you want and work them into the dough. Place in a floured bowl, cover with cling film and leave to rise at room temperature for 45 minutes–1 hour, until not quite doubled in size.

3 Cut the dough into 6 equal pieces and roll them into balls. On a lightly floured work surface, roll out each ball in the shape of a teardrop about 5mm thick. Place on a large oiled baking sheet and set aside at room temperature for 20 minutes.

4 Bake in an oven preheated to 220°C/Gas Mark 7 for 8–10 minutes, until pale golden. Alternatively, fry in oil over a medium heat for a few minutes, turning them over half-way through. Eat straight away, or cool and re-warm in the oven as required.

BREADSTICKS

These keep for ages, well wrapped in a plastic bag. Serve them with a meal instead of a loaf of bread, or as an accompaniment to dips.

Makes 50–60

500g strong white flour, plus extra for dusting

12g fresh yeast

350 lukewarm water

25g olive oil, plus extra for greasing

8g fine sea salt

coarse sea salt or mixed seeds (poppy, mustard and sesame) for the topping

1 Place the flour in a bowl, crumble in the yeast and mix well. Add the water, bring together to form a dough, then tear, roll and turn it for 10 minutes (see page 23, steps 9–11). Add the olive oil and salt, then continue tearing, rolling and turning for a further 5 minutes.

2 Put the dough into a floured bowl, cover with cling film and leave to rise at room temperature for about 1 hour, until doubled in size.

3 Carefully knock back the dough (see page 24, step 16) and cut into 3 equal pieces. Roll them into rectangles about 4mm thick and chill for 30 minutes. Cut each rectangle into long strips about 5mm wide, then roll each strip under your palms to make a thin sausage shape. Place on oiled baking sheets, brush with water and sprinkle with sea salt or mixed seeds. Leave to rise at room temperature for a further 30–40 minutes.

4 Bake in an oven preheated to 160°C/Gas Mark 3 for 20–25 minutes, until pale golden. Carefully transfer the sticks to a wire rack – they break easily – and leave until completely cold.

CARTA DI MUSICA (SARDINIAN CRISPBREAD)

This very thin, brittle bread is named for its resemblance to old parchment, or sheet music paper. Try to make it as thin as possible. It tastes absolutely lovely, but do keep an eye on it when you re-bake it – it burns easily and it's such a shame to spoil it at the last hurdle. I like it served with hummus.

Makes 18

400g strong white flour, plus extra for dusting

350g semolina flour

14g fresh yeast

400ml lukewarm water

1 teaspoon fine sea salt

olive oil for greasing and brushing

2 tablespoons finely chopped rosemary and some coarse sea salt for sprinkling

1 Put the flours in a bowl, crumble in the yeast, then add the water and mix to form a dough. On a lightly floured work surface, tear, roll and turn the dough for 5 minutes (see page 23, steps 9–11). Add the salt and continue tearing, rolling and turning for a further 5 minutes.

2 Transfer the dough to a floured bowl, cover with cling film and leave to rise at room temperature for 1 hour, or until doubled in size.

3 Carefully knock back the dough (see page 24, step 16), then cover and leave to rise again at room temperature for 1 hour, until doubled in size.

4 Turn the dough on to a lightly floured work surface and divide into 18 equal pieces. Roll them into balls using the palm of your hand, then roll out as thinly as possible and put them on oiled baking sheets, spacing them about 1cm apart.

5 Bake in an oven preheated to 220°C/Gas Mark 7 for 2–3 minutes – they should be very pale – then remove and pile them on top of one other (you might want to make 3 or 4 piles so that they don't topple over). Place a chopping board on top to flatten them and leave until cold.

6 Before serving, re-bake for 5 minutes, until crisp, then brush with olive oil and sprinkle with salt and the rosemary. Return to the oven for 1 minute and eat while still warm.

CRUMPETS

What could be nicer than making your own crumpets? But you do need to practise these in order to gain confidence. The most important thing is to get those bubbles on the top to give them their unique appearance and texture.

Makes about 20–24

650ml semi-skimmed milk, plus a little extra

15g fresh yeast

500g self-raising flour

10g fine sea salt

1 rounded teaspoon baking powder

1 teaspoon golden syrup

150g unsalted butter for greasing

1 Heat the milk until just warm. Pour half of it into a bowl, crumble in the yeast, then stir and leave for 15 minutes, until it starts to froth.

2 Put the flour, salt and baking powder in a bowl and mix well. Add the yeast mixture, the golden syrup and the remaining milk. Mix to a thick, smooth batter, then cover with cling film and leave to rise at room temperature for about 1 hour.

3 Butter four 8cm baking rings and a non-stick frying pan large enough to hold them. Put the rings in the pan, place over a low heat and pour a generous tablespoon of batter into each ring. Cook until the top of the batter looks quite dry and the top is covered in little holes. Remove the rings, then turn the crumpets over and cook for another minute. Transfer to a wire rack to cool. Repeat with the remaining batter.

4 Toast the crumpets and serve with butter. I like to sprinkle the melted butter with coarse sea salt.

RYE BREAD WITH RAISINS AND CARAWAY SEEDS

This bread is so good with cheese or pâté and it also toasts well. The seeds are lightly toasted to bring out the flavour.

Makes 2 loaves

1 tablespoon caraway seeds

500g strong white flour, plus extra for dusting

140g rye flour

20g fresh yeast

400ml lukewarm water

12g fine sea salt

75g soft raisins

oil for greasing

1 Heat the caraway seeds in a dry frying pan until it starts to smoke. Transfer to a mortar and crush with a pestle. Set aside.

2 Place the flours in a bowl, crumble in the yeast and add the water. Mix well to form a dough. Turn on to a lightly floured work surface, then tear, roll and turn it for about 10 minutes (see page 23, steps 9–11). Add the salt, crushed caraway seeds and raisins and continue tearing, rolling and turning for a further 5 minutes.

3 Place the dough in a floured bowl, cover with cling film and leave to rise at room temperature for about 1 hour, until doubled in size.

4 Carefully knock back the dough (see page 24, step 16), then cut into 2 equal pieces. Shape into round loaves, place on oiled baking sheets and leave to rise at room temperature, until doubled in size again.

5 Bake in an oven preheated to 220°C/Gas Mark 7 for 15 minutes, then lower the heat to 180°C/Gas Mark 4 and bake for a further 20–30 minutes. The bread is ready if it sounds hollow when tapped on the bottom. Cool on a wire rack.

CORNISH SAFFRON BREAD

I loved eating this when I lived in Cornwall and I always think it looks so pretty with its soft, golden hue. It's important to use genuine saffron strands, as they add flavour as well as colour. Although saffron is expensive, you only need a little. The high fruit content means that the bread rises quite slowly, so be patient with it — it's worth the wait.

Makes 2 loaves

3 pinches of saffron

2 tablespoons boiling water

200ml full-fat milk

25g fresh yeast

50g caster sugar

250g strong white flour, plus extra for dusting

250g plain flour

200g unsalted butter, cut into small pieces, plus extra for greasing

1 teaspoon ground mixed spice

10g fine sea salt

75g sultanas

75g raisins

25g candied mixed peel

1 egg, beaten with 1 teaspoon water, for glazing

1 Put the saffron in a small bowl, add the boiling water and set aside for 15–20 minutes.

2 Heat half the milk until just warm, then add the yeast and half the sugar. Set aside until frothy – this will take about 15 minutes.

3 Place the flours in a large bowl and rub in the butter until the mixture resembles breadcrumbs. Make a well in the centre, then add the yeast mixture, the saffron strands and liquid and the remaining milk. Use your hands to form a dough, then place on a lightly floured work surface and tear, roll and turn it for about 10 minutes (see page 23, steps 9–11).

4 Add the mixed spice, salt, dried fruit and mixed peel, then tear, roll and turn for another 5 minutes, until the dough feels elastic. Place in a floured bowl, cover with cling film and leave to rise at room temperature for 1½–2 hours, or until doubled in size.

5 Butter two 500g loaf tins. Carefully knock back the dough (see page 24, step 16), cut it in half and place in the prepared tins. Leave to rise at room temperature for a further hour, or until doubled in size.

6 Very carefully brush the risen loaves with the beaten egg and bake in an oven preheated to 190°C/ Gas Mark 5 for about 45 minutes. The bread is ready if it sounds hollow when tapped on the bottom. Cool on a wire rack, then serve toasted with butter.

RICH FRUIT BREAD

This is excellent toasted with lots of butter, but it can also be served like a fruit cake. It's packed full of fruit and the ginger gives it a little bit of a kick. Stored in an airtight tin, it will keep for ages.

Makes 2 small loaves

500g sultanas

300g strong white flour, plus extra for dusting

25g fresh yeast

40g unsalted butter, cut into small pieces

40g caster sugar

1 egg, plus 1 egg yolk

about 125ml lukewarm water

5g fine sea salt

125g dried cherries

60g walnuts, chopped

15g stem ginger, crushed

oil for greasing

1 Place the sultanas in a bowl, cover with water and set aside to steep overnight.

2 Put the flour into a bowl, crumble in the yeast, then add the butter, sugar, whole egg, egg yolk and water and mix well to form a dough. Place on a lightly floured work surface and tear, roll and turn it for 10 minutes (see page 23, steps 9–11). Add the salt and continue tearing, rolling and turning for a further 5 minutes.

3 Place the dough in a floured bowl, cover with cling film and leave to rise at room temperature for 1 hour, until doubled in size.

4 Carefully knock back the dough (see page 24, step 16), then place it on a floured work surface. Add the drained sultanas, cherries, walnuts and ginger, and mix until well incorporated.

5 Cut the dough in half and place in 2 oiled 450g loaf tins. Leave to rise at room temperature until doubled in size. This can take over an hour because the loaf is so dense.

6 Bake in an oven preheated to 220°C/Gas Mark 7 for about 45 minutes. The bread is ready if it sounds hollow when tapped on the bottom. Cool on a wire rack.

Traditionally this is a white loaf, but I like to include some wholemeal flour for a more wholesome result. It is effectively a less rich form of brioche. The relatively high fat content means that it will keep for a good 5 days. I make a 3-strand plait, but if you're an expert you can do 4 or even 5 strands.

RICH BREAD PLAIT

To plait the dough, follow steps 7 to 9

MAKES 2 LOAVES

400g strong white flour

200g stoneground wholemeal flour, plus extra for dusting

20g fresh yeast

100g unsalted butter

350ml full-fat milk

1 teaspoon caster sugar

1 egg, beaten

10g fine sea salt

1 egg yolk, beaten with 1 teaspoon water, for glazing

1 Put the flours into a large bowl and crumble in the yeast. Gently heat the butter in a pan with the milk and sugar, until the butter has melted.

2 Allow to cool slightly (until lukewarm), then beat in the whole egg. Stir this mixture into the flour mixture to form a soft dough.

3 Place on a lightly floured work surface and tear, roll and turn it for 10 minutes (see page 23, steps 9–11).

4 Add the salt and continue tearing, rolling and turning the dough for another 5 minutes.

5 Put the dough into a floured bowl, cover with cling film and leave to rise at room temperature for about 1 hour, until doubled in size.

6 Carefully knock back the dough (see page 24, step 16), then cut it in half.

7 Take one half and roll it into a thin baguette shape about 5cm thick and 30cm long.

8 Cut lengthways into 3 equal strands, keeping them joined at the end furthest from you. Repeat this process with the other half of the dough.

9 Plait the 3 strands together, then seal the end nearest to you by squeezing together.

10 Put the 2 plaits on a floured baking sheet and leave to rise at room temperature for about 35 minutes, until doubled in size.

11 Brush the plaits with the beaten egg, then bake in an oven preheated to 200°C/Gas Mark 6 for 30 minutes.

12 The bread is ready if it sounds hollow when tapped on the bottom. Cool on a wire rack.

TIPS AND IDEAS

■ Fresh yeast was always mixed with liquid before use, to check that it was still active, but this dates from the days when you couldn't always rely on the quality. I add it directly to the flour and have never had any problems.

■ The amount of liquid you need to add to the dough can vary slightly according to the brand of flour you use. If it feels too dry, add a little more.

■ For a slightly sweeter loaf, increase the sugar to a rounded tablespoon.

■ You can add flavourings such as sundried tomatoes, dried fruit, herbs or spices after kneading the dough and before leaving it to rise.

■ To make an all-white plait, replace the brown flour with white.

■ If you need more time between kneading the dough and baking it, you can leave it in the fridge for 2–3 hours instead of at room temperature. It will rise perfectly.

■ When plaiting the loaf, I leave the 3 strands attached at one end, as this makes them much easier to work with.

■ Instead of the egg yolk glaze, you could brush the plait with water and then sprinkle it with poppy seeds.

■ To make a sweet glaze for the loaf, add a little Sugar Syrup (see page 232) to the egg yolk before brushing it over. This gives a lovely shiny top.

■ Instead of making a plait, you could shape the dough into a round.

■ This mixture is great made into bridge rolls. Divide the dough into 55g pieces. Roll each one out under your palm into a neat ball, then roll it backwards and forwards into a cylinder about 10cm long. Leave to prove, then dust with flour immediately before putting them in the oven.

TEACAKES

These not only have more substance than most bought teacakes but they are so much tastier. Eat fresh, still warm from the oven, or lightly toast them.

Makes 12

450g strong white flour, plus extra for dusting

50g unsalted butter, cut into small pieces

20g fresh yeast

110ml lukewarm milk

110ml lukewarm water

50g caster sugar

10g fine sea salt

2 teaspoons ground cinnamon

100g sultanas

50g candied mixed peel

oil for greasing

1 egg, beaten with 1 teaspoon water, for glazing

1 Place the flour in a bowl and rub in the butter until the mixture resembles breadcrumbs. Crumble in the yeast, then add the milk, water and sugar and mix to form a dough. Place on a lightly floured work surface and tear, roll and turn the dough for 10 minutes (see page 23, steps 9–11). Add the salt and cinnamon and continue tearing, rolling and turning for another 5 minutes. Place in a floured bowl, cover with cling film and leave to rise at room temperature for 1 hour, until doubled in size.

2 Carefully knock back (see page 24, step 16), then work in the sultanas and mixed peel. Cut the dough into 12 pieces, each weighing 75g. Then roll into balls, flatten slightly with a rolling pin (they should be about 1.5cm high) and place on an oiled baking sheet, spacing them 2cm apart. Leave to rise at room temperature for another 35 minutes, until doubled in size.

3 Carefully brush the teacakes with beaten egg, then bake in an oven preheated to 200°C/Gas Mark 6 for 15–20 minutes. Allow to cool, then split, toast and butter them.

DOUGHNUTS WITH RASPBERRY SAUCE

These make a wonderful pudding, and if you have children standing by while you make them, you will find that the doughnuts disappear as soon as they come out of the pan. They will keep for a day but are best eaten fresh. You can add a little spice, such as cinnamon, to the sugar for coating.

Makes 12

225g strong white flour, plus extra for dusting

a pinch of fine sea salt

40g unsalted butter

1 egg

120ml full-fat milk

15g caster sugar

15g fresh yeast

vegetable oil for deep-frying

caster sugar for coating

For the sauce:

250g raspberries, fresh or frozen

juice of 1 lemon

100g caster sugar, if using fresh fruit

3 tablespoons water, if using fresh fruit

1 Sift the flour and salt into a large bowl. Melt the butter in a saucepan, take off the heat and allow to cool slightly, then whisk in the egg and milk. Stir in the sugar, then crumble in the yeast. Add the milk mixture to the flour and mix to form a dough. Place on a lightly floured work surface and tear, roll and turn the dough for about 10 minutes, until until smooth (see page 23, steps 9–11). Place it in a clean bowl, cover with cling film and leave to rise at room temperature for 1 hour, until doubled in size.

2 Gently knock back the dough (see page 24, step 16), then turn it on to a floured surface and tear, roll and turn it for 2 minutes. Shape into a ball, then roll out to a thickness of roughly 1.5cm and divide into 12 equal pieces. Roll them into balls and place on a baking sheet, spacing them 2.5cm apart, then leave to rise at room temperature for a further 30–40 minutes, until doubled in size.

3 In a deep pan, heat a one-third depth of vegetable oil to 180°C and fry the doughnuts in batches of 4 for 8 minutes, turning them with a metal spoon. Drain on kitchen paper and leave to cool. When cool, roll the doughnuts in caster sugar.

4 To make the sauce, purée the raspberries in a blender with the lemon juice and pass the mixture through a sieve, discarding the seeds.

5 If using frozen fruit, the purée will be liquid enough to serve as it stands. If using fresh fruit, put the sugar and water in a saucepan and bring to the boil, stirring constantly. Simmer for 2 minutes, then allow to cool before adding to the purée.

6 Serve the sauce alongside the doughnuts.

doughnut variation

Traditional Jam Doughnuts – at step 2, after you have made the dough into 12 balls, make a thumb indent in each one, insert a teaspoonful of raspberry jam and close the dough over it to re-form the ball. Continue with the rest of steps 2 and 3.

WHEATEN SODA BREAD

Soda breads are very quick to make, as there's no kneading and rising. The texture of the dough should be like a very thick porridge. If you don't have any buttermilk, add a teaspoon of lemon juice or vinegar to ordinary milk the night before to sour it.

Makes 2 small loaves

360g stoneground wholemeal flour, plus extra for sprinkling (or use extra bran)

120g plain flour

1 teaspoon fine sea salt

1 rounded teaspoon bicarbonate of soda

1 tablespoon bran

1 tablespoon wheatgerm or oatgerm

60g caster sugar

60g unsalted butter, cut into small pieces

about 450ml buttermilk

oil for greasing

1 Place the wholemeal flour in a mixing bowl. Sift in the plain flour, salt and bicarbonate of soda, then stir in the bran, wheatgerm or oatgerm and sugar. Rub in the butter until the mixture resembles breadcrumbs. Make a well in the centre and gradually add enough buttermilk to form a loose dough, rather like thick porridge. The mixing needs to be done quickly but gently.

2 Cut the dough in half and place in 2 lightly greased 500g loaf tins, leaving the surface rough. Sprinkle with wholemeal flour or bran to give a malty surface.

3 Bake in an oven preheated to 220°C/Gas Mark 7 for about 10 minutes, then lower the heat to 200°C/Gas Mark 6 and bake for a further 30–35 minutes. The bread should be firm to the touch, brown and well risen. If a skewer inserted into the centre comes out clean, it is ready.

MEXICAN FLAT BREADS

These flat breads are lightly spiced with chilli. Wrap them around the filling of your choice or serve as an accompaniment.

Makes about 16

500g plain flour, plus extra for dusting

1 rounded teaspoon bicarbonate of soda

1 teaspoon ground mixed spice

½ teaspoon chilli powder

1½ teaspoons fine sea salt

400ml boiling water

2 tablespoons olive oil

1 Put the flour, bicarbonate of soda, mixed spice, chilli powder and salt in a bowl and make a well in the centre. Gradually add the boiling water, mixing with a fork as you do so. Add the oil in the same way. On a lightly floured work surface, tear, roll and turn the dough for 5 minutes (see page 23, steps 9–11), adding a little more water if it feels too dry. Just sprinkle it on and gently work it in. Place in a bowl, cover with cling film and leave to rest at room temperature for 20 minutes.

2 Re-flour the work surface and roll the dough into a long sausage. Cut it into 16 equal pieces, then roll each piece into a ball. Roll out each ball into a circle about 22cm in diameter.

3 Heat a large, dry frying pan. When hot, place a dough circle in it and fry over a medium to high heat until pale speckled brown on both sides. Set aside to cool on a wire rack while you fry the remaining circles in the same way.

BRIOCHE *and* DANISH PASTRIES

This chapter is full of delicious indulgences. Rich, buttery breads like brioche and Danish pastries are not for anyone on a strict diet, but a little treat occasionally doesn't do any harm. A slice of brioche with a cup of good coffee is one of my favourite starts to the day. The Danish pastries may seem like a bit of a fuss, but they are such fun to make and so wonderful to eat. They also freeze like a dream, so if you have time one afternoon you can make a batch and store them in the freezer for later.

A rich, golden brioche is one of the most delicious things you can make. Please don't be put off by the amount of butter in the recipe — it makes 2 loaves and you need only a small slice to feel satisfied. This is one of the few breads where a machine is better than your hands. You could make it by hand, but it will be hard and messy work.

CLASSIC BRIOCHE

To make the brioche dough, follow steps 1 to 4

MAKES TWO 900G LOAVES

250g strong white flour, plus extra for dusting

250g plain flour

20g fresh yeast

40g caster sugar

10g sea salt

6 eggs

250g very soft unsalted butter, cut into pieces, plus extra for greasing

1 egg yolk beaten with 1½ teaspoons water, for glazing

1 Put the flours into a large bowl, crumble in the yeast, then add the sugar and salt and mix well.

2 Now add the whole eggs one by one, mixing all the time (a mixer with a dough hook is good for this). Beat for at least 5 minutes.

3 Add the butter bit by bit, thoroughly incorporating each addition – this will take up to 10 minutes.

4 Beat for a further 5 minutes, until the dough is shiny and slides off the hook.

5 Place the dough on a floured work surface, cut in half and shape into 2 loaves.

6 Transfer them to 2 buttered 900g loaf tins, then cover and leave to rise in the fridge overnight.

7 Remove from the fridge and allow to rest at room temperature for 1 hour.

8 Brush the brioches with the glaze, avoiding the edges as that could inhibit rising. Bake in an oven preheated to 220°C/Gas Mark 7 for 20 minutes.

9 Lower the heat to 150°C/Gas Mark 2 and bake for another 20–25 minutes. Turn on to a wire rack to cool.

TIPS AND IDEAS

■ It's always useful to make a double batch of brioche because it freezes so well. The high fat content means that you can cut off slices from a frozen loaf quite easily.

■ By far the best way to make this dough is in a freestanding electric mixer fitted with a dough hook. You could also use a handheld electric mixer as long as it has a dough hook.

■ You need to be patient when adding the butter. It's always tempting to stop mixing before it has been fully incorporated.

■ This dough has to rise slowly in the fridge overnight because if it was left at room temperature there's a danger the butter would melt. The generous quantity of butter and eggs make it slower to rise than a standard dough in any case.

■ The basic brioche dough can be flavoured in various ways, such as with dried fruit, spices or citrus zest.

■ To give the brioche an extra-shiny top, add a little sugar to the egg glaze used in step 8.

■ You could use this dough to make brioche buns: just shape the dough into 20 balls and place in well-greased bun tins. Prove and glaze as for the main recipe, then bake for about 15 minutes.

■ To make a traditionally shaped brioche, use a special brioche or kugelhopf tin and place the dough in it, keeping a small ball of dough aside. Make an indentation in the top of the loaf with a finger dipped in beaten egg or water, then place the ball of dough on top.

■ Brioche dough can be rolled out into a square, cut into 8cm-wide strips, then scattered with seasonings such as chopped fried bacon, parsley, cheese, olives, anchovies, tapenade, chilli, pesto or ham. Roll up the lengths and leave in the fridge to prove until ready to bake. Brush with egg, then bake at 190°C/Gas Mark 5 for about 15 minutes. Remove and slice. These make delicious nibbles to serve with drinks.

brioche variations

Rum, Walnut and Hazelnut Brioche – prepare the brioche as on page 49, steps, 1–9, but when adding the butter in step 3, also add 50g hazelnuts and 25g walnuts, both coarsely chopped, along with 25g caster sugar and 1 tablespoon rum. This brioche is great with pâté.

Sultana and Cherry Brioche – follow the method on page 49, steps 1–4, using 250g strong white flour, 250g plain flour, 20g yeast, 80g caster sugar, a pinch of salt, 2 eggs and 175g unsalted butter. Stir in 150g sultanas and 125g glacé cherries, then continue as steps 5–7. Glaze and bake in an oven preheated to 150°C/Gas Mark 2 for 45 minutes. Turn on to a wire rack until cold.

Brioche with Gruyère Cheese – roll out half the brioche dough, made as on page 49, steps 1–4, to fit inside a buttered 23cm cake tin. Scatter with 80g grated Gruyère. Form the other half of the dough into 8 balls. Sit one in the middle of the cheese, then dot the others around it. Cover with cling film and leave to rise at room temperature for about 1 hour, then put into the fridge for 2 hours. Glaze and bake in an oven preheated to 220°C/Gas Mark 7 for 20 minutes. Lower the heat to 140°C/Gas Mark 1 and bake for a further 20–25 minutes. Cool on a wire rack before eating warm.

PAIN PERDU

Pain perdu – literally 'lost bread' – is a grown-up way of saying eggy bread. It's sublime made with brioche, but any leftover bread will do.

Serves 6

2 eggs

100g caster sugar

1 teaspoon ground cinnamon

200ml full-fat milk

100ml double cream

zest of 1 orange

6 slices of brioche or bread, cut 2cm thick

60g unsalted butter

1 Put the eggs, sugar and cinnamon into a bowl and whisk together. Add the milk and whisk until very smooth, then stir in the cream and orange zest.

2 Soak the brioche or bread well in the cream mixture.

3 Melt a knob of the butter in a non-stick frying pan and fry 2 or 3 slices of soaked brioche or bread at a time over a medium heat, until golden brown on both sides. Serve with strawberries sprinkled with a few drops of raspberry vinegar.

pain perdu variation

Pain Perdu with Bananas – make the pain perdu as above. Melt 70g unsalted butter in a large, non-stick frying pan over a medium heat and add 4 bananas, sliced diagonally into 4 or 5 pieces. Cook on both sides for 2 minutes. Add 4 tablespoons soft light brown sugar, turn the bananas in it and cook for a further 5 minutes, until brown. Remove the bananas, then add the juice of 1 lemon to create a little sauce. Serve the bananas on the pain perdu and dribble the sauce over them.

CINNAMON ROLLS

These were a childhood treat for me and they're becoming fashionable once again. They taste absolutely wonderful.

Makes 12–14

150g caster sugar

2 tablespoons ground cinnamon

150g raisins

sifted icing sugar for dusting

½ quantity brioche dough (see page 48)

unsalted butter for greasing

1 egg, beaten with 1 teaspoon water, for glazing

For the sweet glaze:

100g granulated sugar

3 tablespoons water

1 Combine the caster sugar, cinnamon and raisins in a bowl.

2 Generously dust a work surface with sifted icing sugar and roll the dough into a rectangle 3mm thick. Spread the raisin mixture over it, then roll up tightly from the long side. Cut the log into slices 1.5cm thick.

3 Place the pastries on a buttered baking sheet, spacing them 2.5cm apart, cover with cling film and place in the fridge overnight or for at least 4 hours. Before baking, allow them to stand at room temperature for 45 minutes.

4 Brush the pastries with beaten egg and bake in an oven preheated to 220°C/Gas Mark 7 for 10 minutes. Lower the heat to 140°C/Gas Mark 1 and bake for a further 10–15 minutes.

5 Meanwhile, make the glaze. Put the sugar and water in a small saucepan and heat gently, stirring to dissolve the sugar. Bring to the boil and boil for 2 minutes, until the mixture is syrupy or registers 110°C on a sugar thermometer.

6 Transfer the pastries to a wire rack and brush with the warm glaze. Leave to cool and set for 30 minutes.

FIG AND RAISIN PANETTONE

You can make this in a flowerpot or even in a heavy-duty brown paper bag, buttered on the inside — turn the top down, if necessary, so that it's not too high. If using a flowerpot, choose an unused one and butter it well. It makes a lovely present. Alternatively, you can buy tall panettone tins or panettone paper liners.

Makes 1 panettone

50g raisins

40ml Sugar Syrup (see Forced Rhubarb and GInger Compote page 278, step 1)

300g plain flour, plus extra for dusting

75g chilled unsalted butter, cut into small pieces, plus extra for greasing

10g fresh yeast

75ml lukewarm skimmed milk

zest of 1 orange

zest of 1 lemon

45g caster sugar

3 eggs

1 teaspoon vanilla extract

4 ready-to-eat dried figs, stemmed and chopped

5g sea salt

1 egg, beaten with 1 teaspoon water, for glazing

For the starter:

50g plain flour

12g fresh yeast

50ml lukewarm water

1 First make the starter. Place the flour in a bowl, crumble in the yeast, then add the water and mix well with a fork. Cover with cling film and leave to stand in a warm place for 45 minutes, or until doubled in size.

2 Put the raisins and syrup into a bowl and set aside to soak for 30 minutes.

3 Place the flour in a large bowl and rub in the butter until the mixture resembles breadcrumbs. Crumble in the yeast, then add the milk, orange and lemon zest, the sugar, eggs, vanilla extract and the starter. Mix well to form a dough, then place on a lightly floured work surface and tear, roll and turn the dough for about 10 minutes (see page 23, steps 9–11). Add the raisins and their syrup, the figs and salt and continue tearing, rolling and turning for a further 5 minutes. Place the dough in a large floured bowl, cover with cling film and leave to rise at room temperature for 1½–2 hours, until doubled in size.

4 Place the dough in a buttered loose-bottomed 20cm cake tin. Set aside to rise at room temperature for a further 30–45 minutes. Brush with beaten egg, then bake in an oven preheated to 220°C/Gas Mark 7 for 15 minutes. Lower the heat to 150°C/Gas Mark 2 and bake for about another 40 minutes, until the panettone sounds hollow when tapped on the bottom. Cool on a wire rack.

EASY PANETTONE WITH APRICOTS AND RAISINS

This is a simplified version of the previous recipe, which means that you don't have to wait so long to eat it. Any leftover panettone will make the best bread and butter pudding – or use it in Pain Perdu (see page 52).

Makes 2 small loaves

650g plain flour, plus extra for dusting

140g chilled unsalted butter, cut into small pieces, plus extra for greasing

35g fresh yeast

150ml lukewarm full-fat milk

75g caster sugar

5 eggs

zest of 1 orange

zest of 1 lemon

2 vanilla pods, split open lengthways

10 ready-to-eat dried apricots, chopped

150g raisins (not large ones)

1 egg yolk, beaten, for glazing

1 Place the flour in a large bowl and rub in the butter until the mixture resembles breadcrumbs.

2 Crumble the yeast into the milk and mix until dissolved. Whisk in the sugar, the whole eggs, lemon and orange zest and the seeds scraped from the vanilla pods, then add to the flour mixture. Mix to form a dough, then place on a lightly floured work surface and tear, roll and turn the dough for 10 minutes (see page 23, steps 9–11). Add the apricots and raisins and continue tearing, rolling and turning for a further 5 minutes.

3 Place the dough in a floured bowl, cover with cling film and leave to rise at room temperature for about 1½ hours. Gently knock back (see page 24, step 16), then shape into 2 loaves and transfer to 2 buttered 500g loaf tins. Cover with cling film and set aside to rise at room temperature for another hour.

4 Brush the top with beaten egg yolk, then bake in an oven preheated to 150°C/Gas Mark 2 for 45–50 minutes, until the panettone sound hollow when tapped on the bottom. Cool on a wire rack.

Croissants used to be my Achilles' heel, but this recipe always works for me. It's relatively simple and as long as you follow it carefully all should be well. Croissants are probably not something you would make regularly at home, but once in a while it's a fantastic experience.

CROISSANTS

To make the croissant dough, follow steps 1 to 12
To shape the croissants, follow steps 13 to 17

MAKES 16

250g strong white flour, plus extra for dusting

250g plain flour

30g caster sugar

2 eggs

250g soft unsalted butter, cut into small pieces, plus extra for greasing

a pinch of sea salt

FOR THE STARTER:

250ml full-fat milk

15g fresh yeast

50g plain flour

1 First make the starter. Heat the milk until lukewarm. Pour into a bowl, crumble the yeast over it and mix well. Sprinkle in the flour and stir to combine well.

2 Cover with cling film and set aside at room temperature for 30 minutes to start fermenting. It should develop lots of little bubbles on top.

3 To make the dough, put the 2 flours into a large bowl, make a well in the middle and add the sugar, eggs, 100g of the butter and the starter.

4 Mix well, then turn on to a lightly floured work surface. Tear, roll and turn the dough until smooth (see page 23, steps 9–11).

5 Put into a floured bowl, cover with cling film and leave to rise at room temperature for about 1½ hours, until doubled in size.

6 Knock back gently (see page 24, step 16), then roll out the dough into a large rectangular strip, about 40 x 25cm and 3–4mm thick.

7 Dot 50g of the remaining butter over two-thirds of the dough, leaving a 2cm border on either side.

8 Fold the unbuttered third of the dough over half the buttered dough, then fold the remaining buttered dough on top to form a parcel.

9 Wrap the dough in cling film and chill for 20 minutes. Then remove from the fridge, unwrap the dough and place it on a lightly floured surface.

10 With one of the open edges of the dough towards you, roll out the dough into a large rectangular strip, about 4–5mm thick.

11 Repeat steps 7–10 twice more. Then fold the dough again, this time without adding butter, turn, roll the dough into a strip and fold once more.

12 Roll the parcel gently to seal. Cover and chill for at least 2 hours before using.

13 Roll out the dough to a rectangle, about 50 x 30cm and 3mm thick.

14 Cut into two 15cm-wide strips, then cut these into triangles. The base of the triangles should be about 10cm wide.

15 Make a 1cm slit in the wide end of each triangle so that the dough can stretch a bit, then roll up so that the point is outside.

16 Place on a buttered baking sheet.

17 Curve the ends together to make crescent shapes, and leave in a warm place to rise for another 30–45 minutes.

18 Preheat the oven to 230°C/Gas Mark 8. Place the croissants in the oven and immediately lower the heat to 200°C/Gas Mark 6. Bake for about 12–15 minutes. Cool on a wire.

TIPS AND IDEAS

■ It's crucial that the butter is the same consistency as the dough, otherwise the dough will tear and the butter will leak out.

■ When you are rolling out the rectangle of dough, keep the edges nice and straight, knocking the sides back into shape with the rolling pin as necessary.

■ In steps 6–10, dust lightly with flour as you go, to prevent the dough sticking, but brush off any excess flour before you fold the dough.

■ In step 15, before you roll up the triangle of dough, flap the point gently to help stretch it; this gives a better shape.

■ After cutting the dough into triangles, you could put a teaspoon of good conserve on each one before rolling it up.

■ Use a very soft brush to glaze the croissants with the egg so that you don't damage them. Professionals often use a spray bottle rather than a brush.

■ Make sure the oven temperature is correct – if the oven isn't hot enough, the croissants won't rise properly during baking.

■ Be sure to cool the croissants on a wire rack rather than leaving them on the baking sheet because they will seep a little butter, which needs to drain off.

■ You can freeze the uncooked croissants on a baking sheet, then transfer them to a freezer bag once frozen. To cook, remove from the freezer, place on a baking sheet and leave for about 30 minutes before baking – they will take 5–10 minutes longer than the time given in the recipe.

croissant variations

Chocolate Croissants – make the croissant dough, roll out and cut into triangles as on pages 57–58, steps 1–14, then place 1 square of chocolate or 3 chocolate chips on each pastry triangle. Roll up and bake as described on page 58, steps 15–18.

Sausage Croissants – make the croissant dough, roll out and cut into triangles as on pages 57–58, steps 1–14. Fry about 6 chipolata sausages, then set aside until cold. Cut them in half and place one half on each pastry triangle. Roll up and bake as described on page 58, steps 15–18.

Cheese Croissants – make the croissant dough, roll out and cut into triangles as on pages 57–58, steps 1–14, then place a teaspoonful of grated Cheddar or Gruyère cheese on each pastry triangle. Roll up and bake as described on page 58, steps 15–18.

CHOCOLATE FILO ROLLS

These are a bit of a cheat, as there's no dough to prepare, but they are utterly delicious. They are also very good made with Nutella, or with the addition of a little orange zest.

Makes 16–20

6 sheets of filo pastry

50g unsalted butter, melted

100g dark chocolate (60–70% cocoa solids), finely grated

icing sugar for dusting

1 Put 1 sheet of pastry on a board, brush with melted butter and place another pastry sheet on top. Cut into rectangles measuring 12 x 10cm.

2 Sprinkle chocolate over the rectangles, leaving a 1cm border around the edges of each one. Roll up the rectangles lengthways, tucking in the ends so that the chocolate cannot escape. You will end up with thin cigar shapes.

3 Repeat steps 1–2 with the remaining pastry.

4 Place the rolls on a non-stick baking sheet, brush with butter and dust with icing sugar. Bake in an oven preheated to 200°C/Gas Mark 6 for 15–20 minutes, until golden brown. Set aside to cool on a wire rack, then dust with more icing sugar before serving.

GREEK BAKLAVA

These make a wonderful dessert or snack and they keep very well. If you are eating them with your fingers, they are very sticky, but you do need to make sure they are drenched in syrup for the best flavour.

Makes 32

200g walnuts, finely chopped

100g almonds, finely chopped

200g caster sugar

2 teaspoons ground cinnamon

1 tablespoon orange flower water

250g melted clarified butter (see tip below)

400g filo pastry

unsalted butter for greasing

For the syrup:

300g granulated sugar

300ml water

4 tablespoons honey

thinly peeled strip of lemon zest

small piece of cinnamon bark

3 cloves

2 teaspoons fresh lemon juice

1 Put the walnuts, almonds, sugar and cinnamon in a bowl. Mix in the orange flower water and 4 tablespoons of the clarified butter, then set aside.

2 Take 1 sheet of the filo and place it in a generously buttered 30 x 20cm baking tin. Brush the pastry with clarified butter, then repeat this process until half the dough has been used.

3 Spread the walnut mixture evenly over the buttered pastry. Cover with the remaining sheets of filo, brushing each one with clarified butter. Heat the remaining butter, then pour it evenly over the top.

4 Using a sharp knife, cut the layered pastry into 5cm squares or diamond shapes. Bake in an oven preheated to 150°C/Gas Mark 2 for 45 minutes, or until the sides are light brown.

5 Meanwhile, make the syrup. Put the sugar, water and honey in a heavy pan and stir over a medium heat until the sugar has dissolved. Add the remaining syrup ingredients, bring to the boil and boil for 15 minutes. Strain and set aside to cool.

6 While the baklava is still hot, slowly pour half the syrup over the top, allowing it to soak in. Serve the baklava with Greek yoghurt, and offer any leftover syrup as an accompaniment.

to make clarified butter

Melt the butter in a small, heavy-based saucepan over a very low heat, until the milky residue has separated. Skim off any froth from the top, pour the clear butter into a jug and leave to cool slightly. Discard the residue in the pan.

CLASSIC DANISH PASTRIES

I use the basic croissant dough on page 56 to make Danish pastries. You can have a lot of fun with different shapes, but try to keep them all roughly the same size so that they cook in the same amount of time. There is no end of possibilities for the fillings — even savoury versions work. The savoury cheese Danish opposite is great with a little salad for a light lunch.

Makes about 12

1 quantity Croissant dough (see page 56)

2 teaspoons vanilla extract

zest of 1 lemon

flour for dusting

unsalted butter for greasing

1 egg, beaten, for glazing

redcurrant jam and/or apricot jam for glazing

toasted flaked almonds or coarse sugar granules for sprinkling

For the marzipan filling:

70g ground almonds

50g caster sugar

50g icing sugar, sifted

1 teaspoon ground cinnamon

1 egg yolk

40ml full-fat milk

2 tablespoons redcurrant jam and/or apricot jam for glazing

toasted flaked almonds or coarse sugar granules for sprinkling

1 Make the croissant dough, as on page 57, steps 1–12, adding the vanilla extract and lemon zest to the 2 flours with the sugar, eggs, butter and starter in step 3.

2 To make the filling, combine the ground almonds, caster sugar, icing sugar and cinnamon. Add the egg yolk, mix well, then loosen with the milk to make a soft dough.

3 On a lightly floured work surface, roll the dough thinly into a 30 x 40cm rectangle. Cut into twelve 10cm squares, then spread a little marzipan filling over each one. Bring the 4 corners into the centre, then place the pastries on a buttered non-stick baking sheet, spacing them about 2.5cm apart. Cover with cling film and set aside to rise a little at room temperature for 30–40 minutes.

4 Brush the top of the pastries with beaten egg and bake in an oven preheated to 200°C/Gas Mark 6 for 15 minutes.

5 Heat the jam until melted, then brush over the pastries while still hot and sprinkle with flaked almonds or sugar granules. Cool on a wire rack.

Danish pastry variations

Cinnamon and Apple Danish Pastries –
peel, core and slice 500g Cox's apples. Place
in a saucepan with 4 tablespoons water and
heat gently until very soft. Add 50g caster sugar,
1 tablespoon ground cinnamon and 20g unsalted
butter, stirring until well combined. Set aside until
cold, then spread over the pastry squares and
allow to rise as in step 3 opposite, then bake and
glaze as in steps 4–5.

Mincemeat Danish Pastries – make the
large pastry rectangle as in step 3 opposite and
spread some mincemeat over it. Roll up into a
long sausage and cut into 2cm slices. Allow to
rise as in step 3, then bake and glaze as in
steps 4–5.

Crème Pâtissière Danish Pastries – put
2 egg yolks, 15g cornflour and 35g caster sugar
in a bowl and whisk well. Heat 150ml full-fat milk
with the seeds scraped from 1 vanilla pod split
lengthways, bring to the boil, then pour on to the
egg mixture, whisking all the time. Pour back into
the pan and stir constantly over a low heat until the
mixture starts to thicken. Stir for another minute,
then transfer to a bowl. Cut the rolled-out Croissant
dough into 10 rectangles about 15 x 5cm. Spread
a tablespoon of the crème pâtissière in the centre
of each one, leaving a 1cm border around the
edges. Brush the border with beaten egg, then fold
the pastry lengthways, press the edges together
and make some shallow decorative cuts around
them. Allow to rise as in step 3 opposite, then
bake and glaze as in steps 4–5.

Lemon and Blueberry Danish Pastries
– follow the recipe for Crème Pâtissière Danish
Pastries below left, replacing the crème pâtissière
with the Lemon Crème Pâtissière on page 100.
After you have spread the crème pâtissière on the
pastry, sprinkle with blueberries, then roll up and
slice like the Mincemeat Danish Pastries left.

Cheese Danish Pastries – omit the vanilla and
lemon zest from the Croissant dough, then roll
out and cut into 10 rectangles about 15 x 5cm.
Sprinkle each one with a little grated Cheddar
cheese and cayenne pepper, leaving a clear
border around the edges. Alternatively, spread
the pastry with coarse mustard or chutney before
adding the cheese. The Onion Compote on page
281 would be particularly good. Brush the border
with beaten egg, roll up lengthways and twist each
roll like a rope. Allow to rise as in step 3 opposite,
then bake as in step 4. Sprinkle with coarse sea
salt before serving.

CAKES

I'm thrilled that home baking has become so popular again. It's comforting to think that we are going back to our baking roots. There was always the aroma of a cake in the oven when I was growing up, and as a small child I used to love scraping out the bowl. I regularly make cakes with my grandchildren and they do exactly the same thing. This chapter covers everything from rich chocolate gateaux to classic Madeira cakes and little, shell-shaped madeleines. Today there are lots of wonderful tins and utensils you can buy for making cakes, which all add to the fun. If you don't have a good kitchen shop nearby, look for suppliers on the internet.

There are so many travesties of this famous gateau, but it really is the most delicious cake in the world when made properly. It's worth splashing out on the best ingredients — top chocolate, good-quality cherry jam and, of course, lovely fresh cream.

CLASSIC BLACK FOREST GATEAU

To make the chocolate cake, follow steps 1 to 9
To make the chocolate curls or shards, follow steps 15 to 17

SERVES 8–10

50g unsalted butter, cut into pieces, plus extra for greasing

6 eggs, separated

180g caster sugar

150g dark chocolate (60–70% cocoa solids), plus 400g for the chocolate shards or curls

150g self-raising flour, sifted, plus extra for dusting

FOR THE FILLING:

2 x 750g jars stoned Morello cherries, drained and juices reserved

75g caster sugar

2 rounded tablespoons cornflour

1 jar good-quality cherry jam

1 tablespoon kirsch liqueur

500ml double cream

20g icing sugar, sifted

1 Butter a 20cm springform or loose-bottomed cake tin, then line the base with baking parchment (see page 19).

2 Melt the butter over a low heat, then set aside.

3 Put the egg yolks and sugar into a heatproof bowl set over a saucepan of simmering water.

4 Whisk until stiff or until the beaters leave a line in the mixture when lifted.

5 Melt the 150g chocolate in a heatproof bowl set over a saucepan of simmering water, taking care that the bowl does not actually touch the water.

6 Carefully fold the melted chocolate into the egg mixture, followed by the flour, then the melted butter.

7 Whisk the egg whites into soft peaks. Fold one-third of them into the chocolate mixture, then fold in the remainder.

8 Pour the mixture into the prepared tin and bake in an oven preheated to 180°C/Gas Mark 4 for about 40 minutes.

9 Set aside to cool in the tin for 15 minutes, then turn on to a wire rack and leave until cold.

10 To make the filling, put the cherries into a saucepan and add enough of their juice to cover. Add the sugar and bring to the boil.

11 Mix the cornflour with a tablespoon of juice from the cherries, then stir into the fruit and boil until it thickens. Set aside until cold.

12 Cut the sponge into 3 layers. Mix the jam with the kirsch until smooth, then spread half the jam on the first layer and top with half the cherries.

13 Put a layer of sponge on top, cover with the remaining jam, top with the remaining cherries and put the final layer of sponge on top.

14 Whip the cream with the icing sugar until stiff and spread the mixture all over the cake.

15 To make the chocolate shards or curls, melt the 400g chocolate in a heatproof bowl set over a saucepan of simmering water.

16 Pour on to a cold surface, such as a marble sheet or glass chopping board, and spread thinly with a palette knife.

17 When nearly set (about 3 minutes), scrape the chocolate away from you with the flat side of a cook's knife or a metal paint scraper to form curls.

18 Transfer the cake to a wire rack and use the chocolate to decorate the top and sides of the cake.

TIPS AND IDEAS

■ This cake will keep in the fridge for 2–3 days and also freezes well.

■ Don't worry if your cake seems quite heavy – it is meant to be, otherwise it wouldn't be able to soak up all the gorgeous flavours from the cherries.

■ Rum or schnapps works well instead of kirsch.

■ Make sure the liquid from the cherries is reduced enough. This not only thickens it but also intensifies the flavour.

■ You could use fresh cherries in season, if you prefer – or even try raspberries or blackcurrants. Poach the fruit with a little sugar and water and thicken the juices with cornflour, as in step 11.

■ The cream needs to be fairly stiff, but do be careful not to over-whip it or it will be unusable.

■ For an even richer cake, you could use chocolate ganache instead of, or as well as, the cream.

■ Melt the chocolate very gently over simmering water, making sure the water doesn't come into contact with the base of the bowl, otherwise the chocolate will 'seize' and become unworkable.

■ When making the chocolate curls, you need to work quickly before the chocolate sets firm. There's quite a knack to doing it, so if the chocolate sets before you've got the hang of it, just scrape it off the board and melt it down again.

■ If you don't have time to make chocolate curls, you can buy white and dark chocolate 'pencils' and cigarellos from online suppliers.

CHOCOLATE TRUFFLE CAKE

This is not a baked cake but a chocolate truffle mixture poured on to a thin almond sponge layer and then chilled until set. It's not overly sweet and makes a wonderful alternative birthday cake.

Serves 12

100g ground almonds

100g caster sugar, plus 2 teaspoons extra for the egg whites

1 egg, plus 1 egg yolk

25g unsalted butter, melted

30g cocoa powder, sifted

3 egg whites

30ml rum or Marsala (optional)

For the chocolate truffle:

350g dark chocolate (60–70% cocoa solids), broken into pieces

700ml whipping cream

35g icing sugar, sifted

1 To make the base of the cake, combine the almonds, 100g sugar, the whole egg and yolk, melted butter and cocoa powder in a large bowl. Whisk the egg whites to soft peaks, then fold in the 2 teaspoons sugar. Use a little of this mixture to loosen the almond mixture, then gently fold in the rest so as not to lose too much air.

2 Line a baking sheet with baking parchment and spread the almond mixture on it in a rough circle. Bake in an oven preheated to 190°C/Gas Mark 5 for about 10–15 minutes, until it springs back to the touch. Set aside to cool on the parchment; it will be spongy rather than crisp.

3 When the base is cold, use a 22cm plastic or stainless steel ring to stamp out a neat circle. Lift the circle on to a plate and brush with a little rum or Marsala, if you wish. (The leftover parts of the base can be frozen and used another time to make little truffle cakes.)

4 To make the truffle, melt the chocolate in a heatproof bowl set over a saucepan of gently simmering water – the bowl must not actually touch the water. Whip the cream and icing sugar very lightly so that the mixture just holds together and will still pour. Whisk in the melted chocolate, then pour over the base, using a spatula to spread it around the sides if you wish. Place in the fridge for at least 4 hours. Serve with Pears in Red Wine with Rosemary Syrup (see page 268).

WARM CHOCOLATE CAKES

An alternative to chocolate fondant puddings, these soft, gooey little cakes are best served warm as a dessert.

Serves 6

160g dark chocolate (60–70% cocoa solids), broken into small pieces

2 tablespoons rum

100g unsalted butter, cut into pieces, plus extra for greasing

3 eggs, separated

60g caster sugar

15g plain flour, plus extra for dusting

1 Place the chocolate in a heatproof bowl set over a saucepan of simmering water, add the rum and butter, then melt over a low heat. Set aside to cool to room temperature, then add the egg yolks.

2 Whisk the egg whites into soft peaks. Reduce the mixer speed and add the sugar and flour, mixing until well incorporated. Fold in the cooled chocolate, then pour the mixture into 6 buttered and floured small ramekins, filling them three-quarters full.

3 Place the ramekins on a baking sheet in an oven preheated to 200°C/Gas Mark 6 for about 10 minutes, or until firm to the touch. Turn out and serve while still warm with Caramel Ice Cream (see page 220).

MADEIRA CAKE

What could be more delicious than a good plain Madeira cake? It's important to use really top-quality unsalted butter to give it flavour.

Serves 6–8

150g soft unsalted butter, plus extra for greasing

150g caster sugar

3 eggs, separated

150g self-raising flour

a pinch of sea salt

1 Whisk the butter until fluffy, then beat in 100g of the sugar. Add the egg yolks one by one, beating between each addition, until the mixture is thick. Sift in the flour, add the salt and fold in.

2 Whisk the egg whites until stiff, then add the remaining 50g caster sugar. Fold a little of this mixture into the flour mixture to loosen it, then mix in the remainder until well incorporated.

3 Butter a 500g loaf tin, then line the base and short sides with baking parchment (see page 19). Pour in the cake mixture and bake in an oven preheated to 180°C/Gas Mark 4 for about 40 minutes, or until a skewer inserted in the middle comes out clean. Turn out of the tin and place on a wire rack to cool. Serve with Pears in Aniseed Syrup (see page 264).

Once you have mastered the basic Swiss roll you can make all sorts of things — including the retro Arctic roll. Quite why they went out of fashion I don't know, as they are so delicious, and since they are basically a fatless sponge, they are lighter and healthier than ordinary sponge cakes.

APRICOT AND MINT SWISS ROLL

To make the basic Swiss Roll cake, follow steps 1 to 13
To assemble and roll the cake, follow steps 16 to 18

SERVES 4–6

3 eggs

100g caster sugar, plus extra for dusting

100g self-raising flour

1 tablespoon milk or water

FOR THE FILLING:

300g ready-to-eat dried apricots

500ml water

6 mint leaves

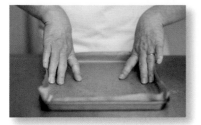

1 Line a 23 x 33cm Swiss roll tin with baking parchment, or make your own paper cake mould (see Tips and Ideas, page 76) and place it on a baking sheet.

2 Place the eggs and sugar in a large heatproof bowl set over a saucepan of simmering water.

3 Whisk with a balloon whisk until the mixture becomes thick and leaves a trail when the whisk is lifted.

4 Remove from the heat and continue whisking for a couple of minutes.

5 Sift half the flour on to the egg mixture and fold in very gently.

6 Sift in the remaining flour and again fold in gently.

7 Add the milk or water and fold again until the mixture is smooth.

8 Pour the mixture into the prepared container and smooth the top with a palette knife.

9 Bake in an oven preheated to 190°C/Gas Mark 5 for 12 minutes, or until firm to the touch.

10 Meanwhile, place a sheet of greaseproof paper larger than the cake on a clean, damp tea towel. Sprinkle with caster sugar.

11 Run a knife around the edge of the baked sponge, then quickly turn on to the sugared greaseproof.

12 Carefully remove the baking parchment from the bottom of the sponge.

13 Place a piece of greaseproof paper on top and put the tin or baking sheet over it until the cake is cold; this should make it moist.

14 Meanwhile, make the filling. Put the apricots, water and mint into a saucepan, bring to the boil, then simmer until all the water has evaporated.

15 Mash with a potato masher, then set aside to cool.

16 Remove the greaseproof paper and tin. Spread the apricot mixture on to the cake. When spreading the filling on the sponge, leave a 1cm border all round.

17 Roll the cake up tightly from the short edge, lifting the undersheet of greaseproof to help you.

18 Slice off the ends of the roll to neaten, then dust the cake with caster sugar before serving with cream, if liked.

TIPS AND IDEAS

■ To make your own paper cake mould, take a sheet of baking parchment measuring 38 x 27cm and fold over 1.5cm all around the edges. Open out the flaps and snip from each corner to the point where the folds intersect. Raise the flaps again, overlap the paper at each corner and secure with sticky tape.

■ Whisking the eggs and sugar over hot water helps to thicken the mixture and give it volume.

■ It's best to use a balloon whisk to create maximum volume but, if you don't feel up to it, a handheld electric beater will also do the job very well.

■ The egg and sugar mixture is thick enough when a trail from the whisk stays on the surface for 2–3 seconds.

■ Sift the flour on to greaseproof paper before adding it to the mixture; this makes it easier to tip in.

■ Keep as much air in the sponge as possible when folding in the flour – I find the easiest way to do this is with a balloon whisk.

■ Don't be tempted to leave the sponge in the oven too long; it should be a very pale golden brown.

■ Before rolling up the sponge, make a small cut, about 1.5cm in, at either side of the short edge nearest to you. This makes it easier to roll it up.

■ Roll up the sponge as tightly as possible and aim for a well-rounded shape. Once you've rolled it up, leave it in the paper for about an hour before cutting, if you have time – this will help it keep its shape.

■ The whole Swiss roll can be covered with chocolate butter icing for a special finish.

Swiss roll variations

Chocolate Swiss Roll – prepare the cake as on pages 75–76, steps, 1–13, but replace 25g of the flour with 25g sifted cocoa powder. Allow the sponge to cool completely. Meanwhile, make a chocolate ganache by bringing 125ml double cream to a simmer, adding 250g dark chocolate, broken into pieces, then cooling for 5 minutes. Stir in 30g unsalted butter, cut into small pieces, and set aside until just warm. Spread over the cake, roll up as shown on page 76, steps 17–18, and dust with icing sugar.

Almond Swiss Roll – prepare the cake as on pages 75–76, steps, 1–13, but replace 30g of the flour with 30g ground almonds. Fold 4 pieces of finely chopped stem ginger into 150ml whipped double cream and spread over the cold sponge. Roll up as shown on page 76, steps 17–18.

Strawberry and Chantilly Cream Swiss Roll – prepare the cake as on pages 75–76, steps, 1–13. Finely slice 250g strawberries and arrange them all over the cold sponge. Make the Chantilly cream by whipping 150ml double cream with 1 tablespoon icing sugar. Spread it over the fruit and roll up the cake as shown on page 76, steps 17–18. To make the cake extra special for a dinner party, soak a little strawberry liqueur into the sponge before rolling it up as before.

Mini Cherry and Almond Swiss Rolls – prepare the cake as on pages 75–76, steps, 1–13. Make a Chantilly cream as described above. Toast 50g nibbed almonds in a dry frying pan until golden. Stone 20 fresh cherries and cut into quarters. Cut the cake into 4 equal pieces. Scatter each piece with nibbed almonds, spread with the cream, then dot with the cherry quarters. Roll up as shown on page 76, steps 17–18, and dust with icing sugar.

Raspberry Swiss Roll – prepare the cake as on pages 75–76, steps, 1–13. Put 250g fresh raspberries in a bowl with 2 teaspoons raspberry liqueur and the zest of 1 orange. Whip 250ml double cream, spread over the sponge, then spoon the raspberry mixture on top. Roll up as shown on page 76, steps 17–18 and dust with icing sugar.

Lemon Cheesecake Swiss Roll – prepare the cake as on pages 75–76, steps, 1–13. Put 100g cream cheese into a bowl with 100ml double cream, the zest of half a lemon and the juice of 1 lemon and beat together. Fold in a quarter of a 397g can condensed milk. Spread over the sponge, then roll up as shown on page 76, steps 17–18, and dust with icing sugar.

Arctic Roll – prepare the cake as on pages 75–76, steps, 1–13, but omit the sugar from the greaseproof when turning the cake out of the tin in step 11. Place 700g vanilla ice cream on a large sheet of cling film and shape into a sausage as wide as the sponge and about 5cm in diameter. Place in the freezer until firm again, then unwrap and place on the sponge widthways. Roll up as shown on page 76, steps 17–18. Store in the freezer until required.

Hazelnut and Chocolate Arctic Roll – prepare the cake as on pages 75–76, steps, 1–13. Spread chocolate ganache (see Chocolate Swiss Roll above left) over the cold Swiss roll and sprinkle with 50g finely crushed hazelnuts. Make a roll of vanilla ice cream as described above. Place on the sponge and roll up as shown on page 76, steps 17–18. Store in the freezer until required. Dust with golden caster sugar before serving.

MARMALADE CAKE WITH BUTTERCREAM ICING

The perfect storecupboard cake. Marmalade is an easy and effective way to brighten up a plain cake mixture.

Serves 6–8

130g soft unsalted butter, plus extra for greasing

130g caster sugar

3 eggs

50ml milk

150g thinly cut marmalade

1 teaspoon bicarbonate of soda

250g self-raising flour

For the buttercream:

80g soft unsalted butter

160g icing sugar, sifted

2 tablespoons double cream

grated zest of 1 orange or 1 lemon and 1 tablespoon of the juice

1 Whisk the butter until pale, add the sugar and beat until light and fluffy. Beat in the eggs one at a time, add the milk, then stir in the marmalade. Fold in the bicarbonate of soda with the flour until well combined.

2 Butter a 20cm loose-bottomed cake tin, then line the base with baking parchment (see page 19). Pour in the cake mixture, make a dent in the middle with the back of a spoon and bake in an oven preheated to 180°C/Gas Mark 4 for about 45 minutes, or until firm to the touch. Cool in the tin for 10 minutes, then transfer to a wire rack until cold.

3 To make the buttercream, beat the butter until very pale and fluffy, then gradually beat in the icing sugar. Fold in the cream and orange or lemon zest and juice.

4 Spread the buttercream over the top of the cake, or cut the cake in half horizontally and use the buttercream to sandwich it together.

CHERRY CAKE

One of the all-time British classics. I prefer to use undyed glacé cherries rather than the brightly coloured ones.

Serves 6

175g soft unsalted butter, plus extra for greasing

175g caster sugar

3 eggs

115g self-raising flour, plus extra for dusting

75g plain flour

a pinch of sea salt

50g ground almonds

175g glacé cherries, chopped in half

1 Butter a 15cm springform cake tin that's about 7 cm deep, and line the bottom and sides with baking parchment (see page 19), taking it about 1cm above the rim.

2 Cream the butter until fluffy, then beat in the sugar. Beat in the eggs one at a time, and continue beating until the mixture is thick. Sift in the flours, add the salt and ground almonds and fold in thoroughly. Finally, fold in the cherries.

3 Pour the cake mixture into the prepared tin and bake in an oven preheated to 180°C/Gas Mark 4 for about 1 hour. The cake is ready when a skewer inserted in the middle comes out clean. Cool in the tin for 10 minutes, then transfer to a wire rack until cold.

---

buttercream variation

Light Buttercream – For a light buttercream, replace 40g of the butter with 40g polyunsaturated margarine. This gives a lighter cream but still has the buttery flavour.

CAKES

79

CARROT CAKE WITH MASCARPONE ICING AND CONFIT ORANGE

I rarely find carrot cakes that I really love, but this one is special – a very soft, moist cake, sweetened with honey, dates and carrots. You don't have to include the icing and confit orange topping, but if you do you can serve the cake as a pudding.

Serves 6–8

250g runny honey

100g carrots, finely grated

180g dried stoned dates, chopped

1 teaspoon ground nutmeg

2 teaspoons ground cinnamon

100g unsalted butter, plus extra for greasing

200ml water

200g plain flour

2 teaspoons bicarbonate of soda

100g walnuts, roughly chopped

3 eggs

For the icing:

200g mascarpone

200g icing sugar

1 teaspoon vanilla extract

200g thick crème fraîche

zest of 1 orange

For the confit orange:

zest of 3 oranges, cut into very fine strips

150g granulated sugar

200ml cold water

1 Place the honey, carrots, dates, spices, butter and water in a saucepan and heat until the butter has melted. Simmer for 5–7 minutes, then set aside until lukewarm.

2 Put the flour, bicarbonate of soda and walnuts into a large bowl. Beat the eggs into the honey mixture, then pour into the flour mixture and mix well.

3 Butter a 20cm springform or loose-bottomed cake tin, then line the base with baking parchment (see page 19). Pour in the cake mixture, level the top and bake in an oven preheated to 180°C/Gas Mark 4 for 45 minutes, or until firm to the touch. Cool in the tin for 10 minutes, then transfer to a wire rack until cold.

4 To make the icing, put the mascarpone in a bowl and sift in the icing sugar. Add the vanilla and beat until smooth. Fold in the crème fraîche and orange zest.

5 To make the confit, place the orange zest in a heatproof bowl and cover with fresh boiling water. Leave for 30 seconds, then drain and refresh in cold water. Repeat twice more, using fresh boiling water each time. Put the sugar and cold water in a small saucepan, bring slowly to the boil, then add the orange zest and simmer for 15–20 minutes, until translucent. Drain and leave to dry.

6 To serve, spread the icing over the cake and garnish with the confit orange.

GINGER CAKE

Ginger cake is wonderful served warm with ice cream or simply eaten with a cup of tea. I like to add quite a lot of ginger, but it's entirely up to you.

Serves 8

unsalted butter for greasing

200g golden syrup from a jar of stem ginger

2 tablespoons syrup

125g muscovado sugar

250g self-raising flour

2 teaspoons ground ginger

½ teaspoon ground cinnamon

1 teaspoon bicarbonate of soda

a pinch of sea salt

2 eggs, beaten

140ml full-fat milk

1 Butter a 22cm square springform or loose-bottomed cake tin and line the base with baking parchment (see page 19).

2 Melt the golden syrup with the stem ginger syrup in a saucepan. Add the sugar and simmer for 1 minute.

3 Sift the flour, spices, bicarbonate of soda and salt into a large mixing bowl. Stir in the ginger syrup, add the eggs and milk and beat well.

4 Pour the cake mixture into the prepared tin and bake in the bottom of an oven preheated to 150°C/Gas Mark 2 for 35–40 minutes. The cake is ready when a skewer inserted in the middle comes out clean. Cool in the tin for 10 minutes, then transfer to a wire rack until cold.

BANANA AND WALNUT CAKE

I can't bear to waste bananas and this is such a quick way of using them up. It works brilliantly.

Serves 6–8

80g soft unsalted butter, plus extra for greasing

150g unrefined golden caster sugar

2 eggs, beaten

500g ripe bananas, mashed

250g self-raising flour, plus extra for dusting

½ teaspoon sea salt

½ teaspoon bicarbonate of soda

100g walnuts, crushed

1 Cream the butter and sugar until very soft. Add the eggs and beat again, then mix in the bananas. Sift in the flour, salt and bicarbonate of soda, mix well, then fold in the walnuts.

2 Pour the mixture into a buttered and floured 700g loaf tin and bake in an oven preheated to 180°C/Gas Mark 4 for about 1 hour. The cake is ready when a skewer inserted in the middle comes out clean. Turn it out of the tin and place on a wire rack to cool.

ORANGE CAKE WITH ORANGE AND CARDAMOM FOOL

This lovely light cake is similar to the ones you get in Turkey. The syrup makes it rich and sticky, but you can omit it if you prefer. The cake doesn't contain any flour, just ground almonds and breadcrumbs. If you cannot eat gluten, omit the breadcrumbs and increase the almonds to 200g.

Serves 6–8

5 egg yolks

145g icing sugar, sifted

grated zest and juice of 1 orange

juice of ½ lemon

3 egg whites

145g ground almonds

80g fresh white breadcrumbs

unsalted butter for greasing

flour for dusting

For the syrup:

150g granulated sugar

150ml water

2 tablespoons orange flower water

For the fool:

grated zest and strained juice of 1 orange

75g icing sugar, sifted

2 teaspoons orange flower water

10 seeds from 1 cardamom pod, crushed

250ml double cream

1 Whisk the egg yolks, sugar and citrus zest and juice until pale and creamy. Whisk the egg whites into soft peaks, then fold them in alternately with the ground almonds and breadcrumbs.

2 Butter a 20cm springform or loose-bottomed cake tin and line the base with baking parchment (see page 19). Pour the mixture into the prepared tin and bake in an oven preheated to 190°C/Gas Mark 5 for about 40 minutes. Turn on to a wire rack and leave to cool until warm.

3 Meanwhile, to make the syrup, put the sugar and water in a pan and bring to the boil, stirring constantly. Boil for 2 minutes, then add the orange flower water. Set aside to cool for 10 minutes. Place the still warm cake on a serving plate, then pour half the syrup over it.

4 To make the fool, add the orange zest and juice, icing sugar, orange flower water and cardamom seeds to the remaining syrup. Bring to the boil, then boil until reduced to 2 tablespoons. Strain and set aside to cool.

5 Whip the cream into soft peaks, then gently pour in the cooled syrup, folding it in as you do so. Serve the fool with a slice of the orange cake.

RUM AND RAISIN FAIRY CAKES

The rum means these are very adult fairy cakes. You can make up the mixture and leave it in the fridge until ready to bake – even overnight.

Makes 12

100g raisins

50ml rum

100g soft unsalted butter

100g caster sugar

2 eggs

100g self-raising flour

½ teaspoon baking powder

1 Put the raisins and rum in a small bowl and leave to soak overnight.

2 Put the butter and sugar into a bowl and cream until pale and fluffy. Beat in the eggs one at a time, then fold in the flour and baking powder and mix well. Finally, stir in the rum and raisins.

3 Line 1 or 2 bun tins with paper cases. Spoon in the batter until the cases are three-quarters full, then bake in an oven preheated to 180°C/Gas Mark 4 for about 25 minutes. Cool on a wire rack.

MADELEINES

You will need a madeleine tin for these in order to get that lovely shell design on each little cake. They are delicious glazed with apricot jam or simply dusted with icing sugar.

Makes about 20

120g caster sugar

3 eggs

1 tablespoon runny honey

4 drops vanilla extract

130g unsalted butter, melted and cooled, plus extra for greasing

130g plain flour

1½ teaspoons baking powder

apricot jam for glazing

1 Whisk the sugar and eggs until light and frothy. Mix in the honey, vanilla and melted butter, then fold in the flour and baking powder.

2 Spoon the mixture into a buttered madeleine tray, filling each indentation two-thirds full. Bake in an oven preheated to 200°C/Gas Mark 6 for about 12 minutes, taking care not to overcook the bottom of the madeleines. They should have a bump on top. Allow to cool slightly, then transfer to a wire rack. Repeat this step until all the mixture has been used.

3 Warm the apricot jam and brush it over the dome of the madeleines while they are still warm.

PISTACHIO POLENTA CAKE

Pistachio paste is available from internet suppliers, but you can also make your own by grinding shelled and skinned pistachios in a food processor.

Serves 10

250g soft unsalted butter, plus extra for greasing

250g golden caster sugar

4 eggs

140g polenta

200g plain flour

2 teaspoons baking powder

50ml olive oil

125g pistachio paste

1 Butter a 23cm springform or loose-bottomed cake tin and line the base and sides with baking parchment (see page 19).

2 Cream the butter and sugar together until light and fluffy. Beat in the eggs one at a time, then add all the dry ingredients, the olive oil and the pistachio paste.

3 Pour the cake mixture into the prepared tin, spread evenly, then bake in an oven preheated to 160°C/Gas Mark 3 for about 45 minutes, or until a skewer inserted in the centre of the cake comes out clean. Turn the cake on to a wire rack to cool. Serve with whipped cream, if you like.

DUNDEE CAKE

A lovely traditional fruit cake that will keep for a good couple of weeks in an airtight tin.

Serves 6–8

225g soft unsalted butter, plus extra for greasing

225g soft light brown sugar

5 eggs

225g self-raising flour

75g ground almonds

½ teaspoon ground nutmeg

350g mixed currants and sultanas

75g glacé cherries, chopped

50g mixed candied peel

50g blanched almonds, split for decoration

1 Butter a 22.5cm springform or loose-bottomed cake tin, line it with baking parchment (see page 19) and tie a double layer of brown paper around the outside to help prevent the cake burning.

2 Cream the butter and sugar until pale. Beat in the eggs one at a time, beating in a little flour between each one. (You need to reserve about 2 tablespoons flour for step 4.)

3 Add the almonds and nutmeg and mix well.

4 Toss the fruit in the reserved flour, then stir it into the almond mixture; the flour coating helps to keep the fruit suspended rather than sinking to the bottom.

5 Pour the cake mixture into the prepared tin, smooth the top and arrange the split almonds on the surface. Bake in an oven preheated to 180°C/Gas Mark 4 for 1 hour, then lower the heat to 160°C/Gas Mark 3 and bake for a further 45 minutes. If, during that time, the top of the cake shows any sign of burning, cover it with a piece of baking parchment. It is ready when a skewer inserted in the centre of the cake comes out clean. Cool in the tin.

BAKED CHEESECAKE WITH EXOTIC FRUITS

Baked cheesecakes are richer and more substantial than ones set with gelatine. Tropical fruit makes this a good winter cheesecake, but in summer you could use summer fruits such as strawberries or raspberries to top it.

Serves 8

300g digestive biscuits

100g unsalted butter, melted and cooled, plus extra for greasing

For the filling:

400g soft cream cheese

200g mascarpone cheese

200g caster sugar

2 teaspoons vanilla extract

2 eggs, plus 2 egg yolks

grated zest and juice of 2 lemons

For the topping:

1 ripe mango, peeled, stoned and sliced

4 passion fruit, halved and pulp seeds scooped out

a little shaved coconut, toasted

1 Crush the biscuits in a food processor or blender, then mix with the melted butter. Spread the mixture inside a lightly buttered 23cm springform or loose-bottomed cake tin and press down evenly with the back of a spoon. Place in the fridge while you prepare the filling.

2 Whisk the cream cheese and mascarpone until light and smooth. Add the sugar and vanilla extract and mix well. Whisk the whole eggs and egg yolks together, then slowly whisk into the cream cheese mixture. Fold in the lemon zest and juice.

3 Spread the lemon mixture over the biscuit base and bake in an oven preheated to 160°C/Gas Mark 3 for about 1 hour, until firm to the touch. Set aside in the tin for 3–4 hours, until cold. It will continue to firm while cooling.

4 Unmould the cheesecake on to a large plate. Decorate the top with the mango slices, dot with the passion fruit and sprinkle with the toasted coconut.

baked cheesecake variation

Baked Blueberry and Vanilla Cheesecake – follow the recipe above, but replace the exotic fruits topping. To make the blueberry topping, place 500g blueberries, the seeds scraped from 1 vanilla pod, split open lengthways, the zest of half an orange, 50g sugar and 2 teaspoons of water in a medium saucepan. Cook over a medium heat until the blueberries start to pop. Allow to cool before spreading over the top of the baked cheesecake.

TARTS
and
PIES

Tarts always look impressive, but they are quite straightforward to make, as long as you allow enough time. Although there are two or three stages, they can be prepared all or partially in advance. You can also freeze empty pastry cases and bring them out as needed. If you master good, crisp pastry, then there's no end to the fillings and variations you can try. For me, a rich chocolate tart or a classic French apple tart represents the height of perfection. This chapter focuses on shortcrust pastry, but most savoury tarts and pies also work well with puff pastry (see page 132).

This is one of the most delicious apple tarts there is. It is quite time consuming to make, as each layer has to be cooked separately, but it really is worth going to this trouble. There is nothing worse than soggy pastry, so don't be tempted to skip the blind-baking stage.

⇒ FRENCH APPLE TART ⇐

To make the basic Sweet Shortcrust Pastry, follow steps 2 to 6
To blind-bake a pastry case, follow steps 11 to 14

MAKES 500G PASTRY AND THE TART
SERVES 6

4 large Cox's apples, peeled, cored and finely chopped

60g unsalted butter, cut into small pieces

1 tablespoon water

grated zest and juice of 1 lemon

75g granulated sugar, or to taste

6 tablespoons Crème Pâtissière (see pages 120–122)

FOR THE SWEET SHORTCRUST PASTRY:

75g caster sugar

2 eggs, 1 separated

1 tablespoon cold water

250g plain flour, plus extra for dusting

125g soft unsalted butter, cut into small pieces, plus extra for greasing

1 egg white, beaten, for glazing

FOR THE TOPPING:

juice of 1 lemon

2–3 Granny Smith apples, peeled, cored and thinly sliced

40g butter, melted

4 tablespoons apricot jam for glazing

1 Butter a 22cm loose-bottomed tart tin.

2 To make the pastry, place the sugar, whole egg, egg yolk and water in a bowl. Mix with a fork, then allow to stand for a couple of minutes.

3 Put the flour in a heap on a work surface and sit the egg bowl on top to make a well.

4 Put the butter in the well and rub with the flour using your fingertips until the mixture resembles breadcrumbs.

5 Add the egg mixture and stir with a fork, then use your fingers and the palm of your hand to form a smooth dough. Do not overwork it.

6 Roll the dough into a log shape, wrap in cling film and place in the fridge for 1 hour before use.

7 When ready to use, remove the cling film. On a lightly floured surface, roll the pastry into a circle.

8 Use the pastry to line the prepared tin, leaving a small overhang, as the pastry will shrink during cooking. Place in the fridge for 1 hour.

9 Meanwhile, prepare the filling. Put the apples, butter and water into a pan and cook very gently until completely soft – about 20 minutes.

10 Add the lemon zest and juice and cook for 2 more minutes. Finally, add the sugar to taste, then set aside to cool.

11 Set the pastry case on a baking sheet. Line with a crumpled sheet of baking parchment and fill with ceramic baking beans, dried pulses or rice.

12 Bake in an oven preheated to 180°C/Gas Mark 4 for about 15 minutes.

13 Remove the paper and baking beans, pulses or rice, then bake the case for a further 5 minutes, or until it is dry and light golden brown.

14 Brush the baked case immediately with egg white, then return to the oven for 1 minute. Remove from the oven and trim the pastry overhang. Set aside until cold.

15 For the topping, place the lemon juice and apple slices in a shallow bowl and cover with water to prevent the apple discolouring.

16 Spread the crème pâtissière in the bottom of the pastry case.

17 Then cover with a layer of the apple purée.

18 Shake the lemon juice off the apple slices. Arrange them on top of the purée in a spiral pattern.

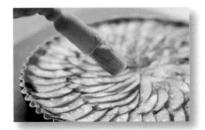

19 Brush the top of the apple slices with the melted butter and bake the tart in an oven preheated to 180°C/Gas Mark 4 for about 30 minutes.

20 Heat the apricot jam until melted, then pass the mixture through a sieve into a bowl.

21 Using a pastry brush, carefully spread the jam over the top of the hot tart in the direction of the apple slices and set aside to cool.

TIPS AND IDEAS

■ If you prefer, the pastry can be made 'all in one', but in this case the butter should be chilled. Pulse the butter and flour in a food processor until the mixture resembles breadcrumbs. Add the whole egg, egg yolk and sugar, and whiz again until a ball of dough forms. Roll it into a log shape, wrap in cling film and place in the fridge for 1 hour before use.

■ With shortcrust pastry, the higher the butter content, the more 'short', or light and crumbly, it will be.

■ Put the log of chilled pastry on a lightly floured surface and flatten it slightly with the palm of your hand. Roll it into a large circle about 2–3mm thick, which is about the thickness of a 10p coin.

■ I always use a ring placed on a silicone mat or on a baking sheet lined with baking parchment because I find it easier to remove the pastry case after baking. If you don't have a ring, use a loose-bottomed tart tin of the size specified.

■ Always butter the inside of your ring or tin.

■ Carefully line the buttered ring with the pastry. If using a tart tin, the edges can be sharp, so it's important to position the pastry accurately first time. To do this, fold the pastry in half, then in half again to find the middle point. Open it out, position it centrally in the tin, then ease it into the curves and up the sides. If using a fluted tin, wrap a small ball of excess pastry in cling film and use this to push the pastry sheet into the curves around the perimeter of the tin.

■ Once you have snugly lined the tin, run the rolling pin lightly over the top to cut off any excess pastry. Don't worry if the pastry splits: sweet pastry is quite forgiving and you can push it together again.

■ You could stir some berries into the cooked apple purée, if you like.

■ Try to slice the apples for the topping as finely as possible. The easiest way to do it is to peel the apple, cut one side off it, lay it down flat and then slice. Repeat with the other sides of the apple.

LEMON-INFUSED CURD TART WITH RASPBERRIES

Based on a classic curd tart, this is served with raspberries arranged on top.

Serves 4–6

½ quantity Sweet Shortcrust Pastry (see page 94)

flour for dusting

150g fresh raspberries for decoration

For the filling:

400g curd cheese

50g soft unsalted butter, plus extra for greasing

110g soft brown sugar

zest of 1 lemon

a pinch of freshly grated nutmeg

1 teaspoon ground allspice

1 egg, plus 1 egg yolk

30g raisins

1 On a lightly floured surface, roll out the pastry and use to line a buttered 15cm loose-bottomed tart tin. Blind-bake as described on pages 95–96, steps 11–14, then set aside to cool.

2 Push the curd cheese though a fine sieve – you should be left with 190g for the recipe.

3 Cream the butter and the sugar, then stir in the lemon zest and spices. Add the whole egg and egg yolk plus the sieved curd cheese, mix well, then fold in the raisins. Pour the mixture into the pastry case, smooth the top and bake in an oven preheated to 160°C/Gas Mark 3 for 40–45 minutes, until pale golden. Set aside until cold.

4 Transfer the tart to a serving plate and arrange the raspberries in concentric circles on top.

PARADISE TART

My mother used to make this, but I believe the recipe comes from Scotland originally. I like to cut it into squares to serve as petits fours.

Serves 6–8

1 blind-baked 22cm Sweet Shortcrust Pastry case (see pages 94–96, steps 1–8 and 11–14)

For the filling:

120g soft unsalted butter

120g caster sugar

1 egg, plus 1 egg yolk

75g ground almonds

50g walnuts

50g sultanas

50g natural glacé cherries, chopped

1 To make the filling, cream the butter and sugar, then add the egg, egg yolk and whole almonds. Tip in the walnuts, sultanas and cherries and mix well.

2 Pour the fruit mixture into the pastry case and bake in an oven preheated to 180°C/Gas Mark 4 for 35–40 minutes, until firm to the touch.

PRUNE, RUM AND CINNAMON TART

This frangipane-based tart is a good storecupboard dessert. Remember that you will need to start it the day before, in order to soak the prunes in rum.

Serves 8

1 blind-baked 22cm Sweet Shortcrust Pastry case (see pages 94–96, steps 1–8 and 11–14)

For the filling:

30 ready-to-eat stoned prunes

rum for soaking

100g soft unsalted butter

100g ground almonds

100g icing sugar, sifted, plus extra for dredging

2 eggs

30g plain flour

1 teaspoon ground cinnamon

1 Put the prunes in a bowl, cover with rum and leave to soak overnight. The next day, drain the prunes, reserving the liquid for another time.

2 Cream the butter, then add the almonds and icing sugar. Beat in the eggs and add the flour and cinnamon. Pour the mixture into the prepared pastry cases and arrange the prunes in a pretty pattern on top. Bake in an oven preheated to 150°C/Gas Mark 2 for about 50 minutes, until firm to the touch and light brown on top.

3 Allow to cool slightly and dredge with icing sugar before serving.

STRAWBERRY TARTLETS

A little box of strawberry tartlets makes such a pretty gift for friends. The trick is not to overfill them. An orange crème pâtissière filling, substituting oranges for the lemons, is very good too. You could also replace the strawberries with other soft fruits, such as raspberries, blueberries and blackberries. This is a richer, more buttery pastry than the one on page 94.

Makes 6

700g ripe small strawberries, hulled

icing sugar for dusting

For the rich shortcrust pastry:

170g cold unsalted butter, cut into small pieces, plus extra for greasing

240g plain flour, plus extra for dusting

2 teaspoons icing sugar

1 tablespoon grated orange zest

a pinch of sea salt

1 egg, separated

1 tablespoon cold water

For the lemon crème pâtissière filling:

4 eggs

grated zest and juice of 2 lemons

125g caster sugar

40g soft unsalted butter

1 First make the pastry. Put the flour into a bowl or food processor, add the butter and rub or process until the mixture resembles breadcrumbs. Add the sugar, orange zest and salt, mix briefly, then add the egg yolk and water and mix or process until a dough forms. Roll into a log shape, wrap in cling film and chill for 30 minutes.

2 Butter six 8cm loose-bottomed tartlet tins. On a lightly floured work surface, roll out the chilled pastry and use to line the prepared tins, trimming the excess with a rolling pin (see Tips and Ideas, page 98). Prick the bases with a fork and prepare the cases for blind-baking (see page 95, step 11). Place on a hot baking sheet in an oven preheated to 200°C/Gas Mark 6 and bake for 15 minutes. Remove the baking beans, pulses or rice and paper, brush the cases with egg white and bake for another 5 minutes, until golden. Set aside until cold, then remove the pastry cases from the tins.

3 To make the filling, beat the eggs in a large bowl until pale. Put the lemon zest and juice in a saucepan with the sugar, bring to the boil, then beat in the butter. Add this mixture to the eggs, then return to the pan and slowly bring to a simmer, whisking all the time. Strain and set aside until cold.

4 Spread a rounded tablespoon of the lemon crème pâtissière in each pastry case. Arrange the strawberries on top and dust with icing sugar. Any leftover crème pâtissière can be frozen for future use.

FIG AND WALNUT TART

The advantage of dried figs is that you can use them all year round, but this lovely tart is arguably even nicer made with fresh figs in season.

Serves 6–8

1 blind-baked 23cm Sweet Shortcrust Pastry case (see pages 94–96, steps 1–8 and 11–14)

For the filling:

6 ready-to-eat dried figs, stemmed and finely diced

200g walnuts, chopped

50g soft unsalted butter

80g caster sugar

50g ground almonds

25g plain flour

3 eggs, beaten

60g honey

zest of 2 oranges

200ml double cream

1 Put the figs and walnuts into a bowl, mix well, then tip into the pastry case.

2 In the same bowl, cream the butter and sugar until pale. Add the almonds, flour and eggs and mix well. Stir in the honey and orange zest, then fold in the double cream.

3 Pour the mixture into the pastry case and bake in an oven preheated to 160°C/Gas Mark 3 for 40–45 minutes, until golden. Serve cold.

FRUIT AND NUT BUTTER TART

This is the famous Scottish Ecclefechan tart. Traditionally the pastry is not pre-baked, but if you would like a crisper base, do bake it blind first (see pages 95–96, steps 11–14).

Serves 6–8

1 uncooked 22cm Sweet Shortcrust Pastry case (see pages 94–95, steps 1–8), chilled

For the filling:

350g mixed dried fruit

3 tablespoons rum

2 eggs

180g soft light brown sugar

1 tablespoon red wine vinegar

150g unsalted butter, melted and cooled

100g chopped walnuts

1 To make the filling, put the dried fruit and rum in a bowl and set aside to soak for 30 minutes.

2 Whisk the eggs and sugar with the vinegar, then whisk in the melted butter. Add the walnuts, dried fruit and rum and mix well. Transfer to a food processor and pulse to a coarse texture (you do not want a purée).

3 Fill the chilled pastry case with the fruit and nut mixture and bake in an oven preheated to 190°C/Gas Mark 5 for 30–35 minutes. Serve hot or cold.

RICH AND CREAMY CHOCOLATE TART

This is a very rich tart indeed, made with a classic chocolate ganache.

Serves 8

220g dark chocolate (60–70% cocoa solids),
broken into pieces

25g unsalted butter, cut into pieces

400ml double cream, at room temperature

20g icing sugar, sifted

For the chocolate pastry:

150g soft unsalted butter, plus extra for
greasing

90g icing sugar, sifted

25g cocoa powder, sifted

1 egg, plus 1 egg yolk

2 tablespoons water

270g plain flour, sifted, plus extra for dusting

1 First make the pastry. Beat the butter in a bowl until pale. Add the icing sugar and cocoa powder and stir well. Beat in the whole egg, egg yolk and water until well incorporated. Finally, fold in the flour until a sticky dough forms. Flour your hands and shape the dough into a ball, then wrap it in cling film. Place in the fridge for 3–4 hours.

2 Butter a 22cm loose-bottomed tart tin. Place the chilled pastry on a lightly floured work surface and roll into a circle about 28cm in diameter. Use to line the prepared tin, tucking it well into the corners and leaving the excess pastry overhanging the sides. Chill for 30 minutes.

3 Prick the base of the pastry all over with a fork, then prepare for blind-baking as shown on page 95, step 11. Bake in an oven preheated to 180°C/Gas Mark 4 for 15–20 minutes, then remove the baking beans, pulses or rice and return the pastry case to the oven for a further 5 minutes, until light golden brown.

4 Meanwhile, place the chocolate and butter in a heatproof bowl set over a saucepan of simmering water and allow to melt. Make sure the mixture does not get hotter than 55°C, otherwise the chocolate will become grainy. Set aside to cool down to about room temperature.

5 Trim the excess pastry off the cooled case. Pour the cream into a bowl, add the icing sugar and mix well. Whisk into the chocolate mixture, then pour into the pastry case. Place the tart in the fridge and cool for about 4 hours before serving.

WARM CHOCOLATE TART

The most gorgeous, unctuous chocolate tart, this will feed any chocolate addiction.

Serves 8

1 blind-baked 22cm Sweet Shortcrust Pastry case (see pages 94–96, steps 1–8 and 11–14)

For the filling:

200g unsalted butter, cut into pieces

200g dark chocolate (60–70% cocoa solids), broken into pieces

2 eggs, plus 3 egg yolks

80g caster sugar

1 Melt the butter and chocolate together in a heat-proof bowl set over a saucepan of simmering water. Set aside to cool down to about room temperature.

2 Whisk together the whole eggs, egg yolks and sugar until just combined, then fold the melted chocolate mixture into the egg mixture and pour into the pastry case.

3 Bake in an oven preheated to 150°C/Gas Mark 2 for about 30 minutes. The filling should be smooth and creamy with a slight wobble, just setting. Set aside to rest in a warm place for 30 minutes before serving.

TREACLE TART

You just cannot beat a good treacle tart. Remember to be generous with the lemon juice, to offset the sweetness.

Serves 8

1 blind-baked 22cm Sweet Shortcrust Pastry case (see pages 94–96, steps 1–8 and 11–14)

For the filling:

400g golden syrup

1 tablespoon water

grated zest and juice of ½ lemon

150g fresh white breadcrumbs

1 Combine all the filling ingredients in a bowl, then pour the mixture into the prepared pastry case.

2 Bake in an oven preheated to 180°C/Gas Mark 4 for about 20 minutes, until golden. Cool to room temperature, then serve with cream.

treacle tart variation

Brioche Treacle Tart – follow the recipe above, but use crumbled Sultana and Cherry Brioche (see page 51) instead of ordinary white breadcrumbs.

BANOFFEE PIE

I have had dreadful banoffee pies in my time — over-sweet and with too much cream. When it's made properly it's absolutely wonderful. This one is drizzled with a dark chocolate sauce, which takes the edge off the sweetness.

Serves 6–8

80g unsalted butter

75g caster sugar

200ml caramelised condensed milk (available from supermarkets)

3 large bananas, sliced

50g pecans, roughly chopped

For the base:

200g digestive biscuits

50g pecans

80g unsalted butter, melted and cooled

For the topping:

250ml double cream

65g icing sugar, sifted

For the chocolate sauce:

100g dark chocolate (60–70% cocoa solids), broken into pieces

25g unsalted butter

1 tablespoon double cream

1 Line the sides of a 22cm loose-bottomed tart tin with baking parchment (see page 19).

2 To make the base, crush the digestives and pecans into fine crumbs, then stir in the melted butter. Spoon the mixture into the tart tin and press evenly over the base and slightly up the sides. Chill in the fridge for 30 minutes.

3 Meanwhile, make the filling. Slowly melt the butter with the caster sugar in a saucepan, stirring all the time, and bring to the boil. Continue boiling until it becomes a caramel colour, then fold in the condensed milk and take off the heat.

4 Fold the bananas and pecans into the caramel sauce, then spread the mixture over the biscuit base. Chill in the fridge for 1 hour.

5 To make the topping, whip the cream to soft peaks and fold in the icing sugar. Spoon this mixture over the banana filling.

6 To make the sauce, melt the chocolate in a heatproof bowl set over a saucepan of simmering water (make sure the bowl does not actually touch the water). Fold in the butter, then stir in the cream. Drizzle the sauce over the pie and serve.

RHUBARB AND MASCARPONE TARTS

Used forced rhubarb for this, if possible, because it has the most beautiful colour. Serve with Ginger Ice Cream (see page 224).

Serves 4

500g forced rhubarb

150g caster sugar

grated zest and juice of 1 orange

For the base:

100g soft unsalted butter, plus extra for greasing

100g caster sugar

100g ground almonds

For the mascarpone filling:

250g mascarpone

2 teaspoons icing sugar

1 tablespoon Grand Marnier liqueur

1 Start by making the base. Cream the butter and sugar until soft and pale, then mix in the ground almonds. Divide the mixture into 4 equal pieces and roll each one into a ball. Cover with cling film and chill for 30 minutes.

2 Generously butter 4 loose-bottomed 8cm tart tins. Put an almond ball in each tin and press with your fingers to spread it over the base and up the sides. Bake in an oven preheated to 150°C/Gas Mark 2 for 25–30 minutes, until golden brown. Cool in the tins for 15 minutes, then carefully transfer to a wire rack and leave until cold.

3 Cut the rhubarb into 6cm chunks. Place in a shallow baking tin, sprinkle with the sugar and orange zest and juice and mix well. Bake in the oven for about 15 minutes, until just cooked; it must still have some bite. Set aside until cold.

4 Mix the mascarpone with the icing sugar and Grand Marnier. Divide equally between the pastry cases, then top with a neat pile of rhubarb.

PECAN PIE

This American classic is not seen on restaurant menus as often as it used to be, but it definitely deserves a revival.

Serves 6

1 blind-baked 22cm Sweet Shortcrust Pastry case (see pages 94–96, steps 1–8 and 11–14)

For the filling:

250g pecan halves

3 eggs

100g maple syrup

1 teaspoon vanilla extract

100g unsalted butter, melted and cooled

130g soft dark brown sugar

1 Crush 175g of the pecans and sprinkle them over the base of the pastry case.

2 Whisk the eggs until pale. Add the maple syrup, vanilla, melted butter and sugar and mix well. Pour into the pastry case and bake in an oven preheated to 180°C/Gas Mark 4 for 30 minutes. Lower the temperature to 150°C/Gas Mark 2 and bake for a further 10 minutes, until golden brown. Set aside until cold.

3 Arrange the remaining pecan halves in a pretty pattern on top of the warm pie, then set aside until completely cold. Serve with whipped cream, adding a dash of rum to it, if you like.

CLASSIC APPLE PIE

Don't use a ceramic dish for this — the traditional metal pie dishes are best. You can't beat an old-fashioned pie tin filled to the brim with Bramley apples. I think it is one of the best British dishes of all time. Serve with thick clotted cream or with custard.

Serves 6–8

250g plain flour, plus extra for dusting

140g cold unsalted butter, cut into small pieces, plus extra for greasing

1 tablespoon caster sugar

4 tablespoons cold water

1 egg beaten with 1 tablespoon milk, for glazing

For the filling:

4 Bramley apples, peeled and cored

2 tablespoons apple juice or lemon juice

120g caster sugar, plus extra for dusting

50g unsalted butter

1 First make the filling. Cut the apples into 8–10 pieces, place in a saucepan with the apple or lemon juice and sugar and bring to a simmer over a low heat. Cook gently for 15–20 minutes. Fold in the butter, then set aside to cool.

2 Put the flour into a bowl or food processor, add the butter and rub together or pulse until the mixture resembles breadcrumbs. Add the sugar and water and mix or process into a dough.

3 Cut the pastry in half, place it on a lightly floured work surface and roll out to fit a buttered 20cm pie dish, leaving it slightly overhanging the sides. Roll out the other half, ready to put over the top.

4 Fill the lined pie dish with the cooled apple, then brush the beaten egg around the edge. Place the pastry lid over the top and press all around the dish to make sure it's well sealed.

5 Using a sharp knife, trim off the excess pastry. Brush the top with beaten egg, cut a small steam-hole, about 5mm in diameter, in the middle of the pastry, then bake in an oven preheated to 200°C/ Gas Mark 6 for 30–35 minutes, until golden. Dust with caster sugar before serving.

apple pie variation

Apple and Rhubarb Pie – make the basic pie as above, using just 3 Bramley apples and cooking them with 500g chopped forced rhubarb and 250g caster sugar.

ONION TART

Savoury tarts are absolutely delicious and brilliant served with salad for lunch or a light supper. The trick with this tart is to make sure the onions are well caramelised. You need to be patient, as it cannot be hurried, but it will add flavour and richness to the filling. I always include lots of herbs in this.

Serves 6

2 Spanish onions, finely sliced

olive oil

1 teaspoon caster sugar

1 tablespoon fresh thyme leaves or
2 teaspoons dried thyme

100g cream cheese

2 eggs, plus 2 egg yolks

300ml double cream

1 teaspoon smoked paprika

sea salt and black pepper

For the savoury shortcrust pastry:

200g plain flour, plus extra for dusting

75g unsalted butter, cut into small pieces, plus extra for greasing

25g lard, cut into small pieces

1 egg

1 egg white, beaten, for glazing

1 First make the pastry. Put the flour, butter and lard in a large bowl and rub together until the mixture resembles fine breadcrumbs. Add the whole egg and use a round-bladed knife in a cutting motion to mix until a dough forms. Shape into a smooth ball, then wrap in cling film and chill for 30 minutes.

2 Roll out the pastry on a lightly floured work surface and use to line a buttered 22cm loose-bottomed tart tin. Prick the base with a fork and prepare the case for blind-baking (see page 95, steps 11). Place in an oven preheated to 200°C/Gas Mark 6 and bake for 15 minutes. Remove the baking beans, pulses or rice and paper, brush the cases with egg white and bake for another 5 minutes, until golden. Set aside until cold.

3 To make the filling, fry the onions in a little oil in a large frying pan on a low heat until very soft – this can take 30–40 minutes. Add the sugar and thyme, season with salt and pepper and allow to cool.

4 Put the cream cheese, whole eggs, egg yolks and cream into a bowl and beat until soft and smooth. Arrange the onion evenly inside the pastry case and pour the egg mixture over it. Sprinkle with the smoked paprika, then bake in an oven preheated to 200°C/Gas Mark 6 for 15 minutes. Lower the heat to 150°C/Gas Mark 2 and bake for a further 15–20 minutes, or until golden brown.

ROAST TOMATO TART

This is a great way to make a tart without a tart tin. It looks a little bit like a large vol-au-vent. You could make 4 individual tarts, if you like, using 11cm and 10cm cutters.

Serves 6

1 quantity Savoury Shortcrust Pastry (see opposite)

flour for dusting

1 egg, beaten, for glazing

For the filling:

3 tablespoons double cream or crème fraîche

3 tablespoons Dijon mustard

30 cherry tomatoes, sliced

leaves from 4 sprigs of thyme

olive oil for drizzling and greasing

sea salt and black pepper

1 Place the pastry on a lightly floured work surface and roll it into a circle about 24cm in diameter. Place a 23cm tart tin or saucepan lid on the pastry and cut around it. Now place a 22cm tart tin or saucepan lid in the middle of the pastry circle and cut around that to create a narrow border.

2 Transfer the inner circle to an oiled non-stick baking sheet and brush a 1cm border of beaten egg around the edge. Lift up the narrow pastry border and sit it on the glazed circle, cutting it to fit neatly.

3 To make the filling, combine the cream or crème fraîche and mustard in a bowl, then spread the mixture over the inner pastry circle. Arrange the tomato slices on it, season with salt and pepper and scatter the thyme leaves over the top. Bake in an oven preheated to 190°C/Gas Mark 5 for about 15 minutes, until slightly caramelised. Drizzle the tart with a little olive oil and serve warm or cold.

SALMON AND TARRAGON TART

Fresh salmon makes a lovely summery tart – though I have been known to use canned salmon in this. Use whichever you have available.

Serves 6–8

1 blind-baked 22cm Savoury Shortcrust Pastry case (see opposite, steps 1–2)

For the filling:

450g fresh salmon fillet

a few lemon slices

3 eggs, plus 1 egg yolk

100g cream cheese

350ml double cream

leaves from 2 large sprigs of tarragon, chopped, or 2 teaspoons dried tarragon

sea salt and black pepper

1 Put the salmon on a sheet of foil, add salt, pepper and the lemon slices, then seal tightly. Place the parcel on a baking sheet in an oven preheated to 180°C/Gas Mark 4 and bake for 15–20 minutes. Set aside to cool.

2 Put the whole eggs, egg yolk and cream cheese into a bowl and whisk until smooth. Mix in the cream, season well with salt and pepper, then stir in the tarragon.

3 Flake the salmon into the pastry case, then pour in the cream mixture. Bake in an oven preheated to 200°C/Gas Mark 6 for 15 minutes. Lower the heat to 150°C/Gas Mark 2 and cook for another 10–15 minutes, until pale golden brown. Cool slightly before serving.

CARAMELISED ONION, BLUE CHEESE AND WALNUT TART

I like to make this into individual tarts too. You can play about with different cheeses, but be sure to choose a strong one. Gruyère works well.

Serves 4

1 blind-baked 22cm Savoury Pastry case (see page 110, steps 1–2)

For the filling:

2 tablespoons olive oil

30g unsalted butter

4 red onions, finely sliced

40g caster sugar

20 walnut halves, toasted

150g Yorkshire blue cheese, crumbled

sea salt and black pepper

1 Put the oil and butter into a large frying pan, add the onions and cook on a low heat for 30 minutes. Increase the heat a little, add the sugar and cook for a further 5–10 minutes. Season well with salt and pepper.

2 To assemble the tart, spoon the caramelised onion into the pastry case, arrange the walnuts over the surface and scatter the blue cheese on top.

3 Bake in an oven preheated to 180°C/Gas Mark 4 for 15–20 minutes, until pale golden brown.

BEETROOT AND GOATS' CHEESE TART

This contains a whole head of garlic, but the flavour mellows during roasting.

Serves 4

1 blind-baked 22cm Savoury Shortcrust Pastry case (see page 110, steps 1–2)

For the filling:

4 medium beetroot, peeled and cut into 5mm dice

80g unsalted butter, cut into pieces

5 sage leaves, roughly chopped

1 whole garlic bulb, separated into cloves but not peeled

2 red onions, finely diced

3 tablespoons olive oil

1 teaspoon balsamic vinegar

2 eggs

150ml double cream

200g goats' cheese, sliced

1 teaspoon thyme leaves

sea salt and black pepper

1 Place the beetroot in a gratin dish with the butter, sage and garlic. Cover with foil and bake in an oven preheated to 200°C/Gas Mark 6 for 1 hour, until soft. Meanwhile, put the onions and oil in a pan and cook very gently until soft – up to 20 minutes.

2 Stir the onions into the beetroot mixture, add the vinegar and squeeze in the softened garlic from the skins. Season well and set aside to cool.

3 Whisk the eggs and cream together in a bowl.

4 Put the beetroot and onion mixture into the cooled pastry case. Arrange the cheese slices on top, reserving a few for the topping. Pour over the egg mixture and top with the thyme and reserved cheese. Bake in an oven preheated to 180°C/Gas Mark 4 for 20 minutes, until pale golden brown.

LEEK, BLACK PUDDING AND OATMEAL TART

Someone said to me that this is a really a breakfast tart, with its bacon, eggs and black pudding. The oatmeal makes delicious, very workable pastry. You can buy porridge oats and grind them in a food processor, if necessary. I adore black pudding, with my particular favourite being from Stornoway, on the Isle of Lewis in the Outer Hebrides.

Serves 6

30g unsalted butter, plus extra for greasing

300g leeks, finely sliced

175ml double cream

2 eggs

2 tablespoons chopped parsley

½ teaspoon dried marjoram

60g smoked Cheddar, grated

3 dry-cured rashers of streaky bacon, chopped

240g black pudding, skinned and cut into chunks

sea salt and black pepper

For the oatmeal pastry:

120g plain flour, plus extra for dusting

120g ground oats

a good pinch of fine sea salt

120g unsalted butter or lard, or 50:50 mixture, cut into small pieces

1 egg, beaten, for glazing

1 egg white for brushing

1 First make the pastry. Put the flour, oats and salt into a bowl, add the fat and rub together until the mixture resembles breadcrumbs. Add the beaten whole egg, mixing until a smooth dough forms. Wrap in cling film and chill for 30 minutes.

2 Place the dough on a lightly floured work surface and roll into a circle large enough to line a buttered 22cm loose-bottomed tart tin. Prick the base with a fork, then blind-bake as described on page 95–96, steps 11–14.

3 To make the filling, put the butter and leeks in a pan and cook gently until soft. Beat in the cream, eggs, herbs and half the cheese. Season with salt and pepper, then pour the mixture into the prepared pastry case.

4 Fry the bacon until the fat runs. Add the black pudding and fry gently to absorb the bacon flavour. Sprinkle the black pudding and bacon over the leek filling and push down into the mixture. Scatter the remaining cheese over the top and bake in an oven preheated to 180°C/Gas Mark 4 for 30–35 minutes.

SCRAMBLED EGG AND ANCHOVY PETITS FOURS

The cornflour in this pastry helps prevent it shrinking, making it ideal for tiny petits fours cases.
The filling does have to be made at the last minute, but really doesn't take very long to do.

Makes 50

4 eggs

15g butter

1 tablespoon double cream

8 preserved anchovies, cut into fine strips

sea salt and black pepper

For the petit fours pastry:

75g unsalted butter, cut into small pieces, plus extra for greasing if necessary

225g plain flour, plus extra for dusting

20g cornflour

1 egg, beaten

25ml milk

---

petit four variations

Crab Petits Fours – put 250g white crabmeat into a bowl. Add 3 tablespoons mayonnaise, 1 rounded teaspoon finely chopped dill, ¼ skinned, deseeded and finely diced red pepper and 1 rounded tablespoon chopped chives. Mix well and season to taste with salt and pepper. Fill the pastry cases and add a chervil sprig to each one.

Tuna Tartar Petits Fours – finely dice 500g very fresh tuna and place in a bowl with 2 skinned, deseeded and chopped tomatoes, 1 thinly sliced spring onion, 1 tablespoon toasted sesame oil, 1 tablespoon teriyaki sauce and 4 tablespoons chopped coriander. Mix well and chill for 1 hour. Stir in 1 tablespoon sesame seeds and the juice of 1 lime and mix. Fill the pastry cases and sprinkle with chopped chives.

---

1 First make the pastry. Place the flour and butter in a bowl and rub together until the mixture resembles breadcrumbs. Stir in the cornflour, then add the egg and milk and mix into a smooth dough. Roll into a log shape, wrap in cling film and chill for 30 minutes.

2 Place the dough on a lightly floured work surface and roll out to a thickness of 2mm. Arrange rows of individual petit fours tins on the work surface, buttering them first if they are not non-stick. Lay the pastry over the top, then use a small cling film-wrapped ball of pastry to push the pastry into the tins. Run a rolling pin over the top to remove the excess pastry.

3 To blind-bake these little cases, stack them in threes and put an empty tin in the top one of each stack. Place on a baking sheet and bake in an oven preheated to 180°C/Gas Mark 4 for about 15 minutes.

4 Beat the eggs in a bowl and season well with salt and pepper.

5 Melt the butter in a frying pan, add the eggs and gently scramble them. Just before they thicken, add the cream. Fill the pastry cases with the scrambled egg and top each one with an anchovy strip.

SPINACH AND QUAIL'S EGG TARTLETS

These little tarts also make delicious canapés. Just double the number of quail's eggs and cut each tart into quarters.

Makes four 10cm tartlets

30g goats' cheese

2 hen's eggs

2 tablespoons double cream

1 tablespoon grated Parmesan cheese

freshly grated nutmeg

400g cooked spinach, well drained

8 quail's eggs

4 sprigs of chervil

sea salt and black pepper

For the pastry:

150g plain flour, plus extra for dusting

½ teaspoon sea salt

30g unsalted butter, cut into small pieces, plus extra for greasing

1 small egg, beaten

1 egg white, beaten, for glazing

1 First make the pastry. Put the flour and salt into a bowl, add the butter and rub together until the mixture resembles breadcrumbs. Mix in the whole egg, then add just enough cold water to form a dough. Cover in cling film and chill for 30 minutes.

2 Meanwhile, put the goats' cheese, salt and pepper into a blender or food processor and whiz to a purée.

3 Whisk the hen's eggs in a bowl, add the cream and Parmesan, then season with salt, pepper and a little nutmeg. Fold in the spinach.

4 Butter four 10cm loose-bottomed tartlet tins. On a lightly floured work surface, roll out the chilled pastry and use to line the prepared tins. Prick the bases with a fork and prepare the cases for blind-baking (see page 95, step 11). Place on a hot baking sheet in an oven preheated to 200°C/Gas Mark 6 and bake for 12–15 minutes. Remove the baking beans, pulses or rice and paper, brush the cases with egg white and bake for a few more minutes, until crisp and golden.

5 Fill the pastry cases with the spinach mixture and smooth the surface. Season with salt and pepper and bake in an oven preheated to 160°C/Gas Mark 3 for 15 minutes.

6 Meanwhile, boil the quail's eggs for 2 minutes. Cool in iced water, peel off the shells and cut in half.

7 Remove the tarts from the tins and place 2 halves of quail's egg on top of each one before serving.

CORNISH PASTIES

I was brought up on my mother's Cornish pasties. She used to make rather large ones and so these are pretty generous. You could make 8 smaller pasties, if you prefer.

Makes 4 large pasties

600g skirt beef, cut into fine strips

200g potato, finely sliced

150g onion, finely sliced

150g swede, finely sliced

1 egg, beaten, for glazing

5g sea salt

black pepper

For the pastry:

500g plain flour, plus extra for dusting

75g unsalted butter, cut into small pieces

75g lard, cut into small pieces

170ml cold water

1 teaspoon fine sea salt

1 First make the pastry. Put the flour into a bowl and rub in the butter and lard until the mixture resembles rough breadcrumbs. Add the water and salt and mix until a smooth dough forms. Wrap in cling film and chill for about 30 minutes.

2 To make the filling, combine the beef and vegetables in a bowl. Add the salt and pepper and mix well.

3 Place the chilled dough on a lightly floured work surface, cut into 4 equal pieces, depending on the size of pasty you would like, and roll each piece into a circle 25cm in diameter. Place equal amounts of the meat mixture in the centre of each circle. Brush beaten egg all around the filling, then lift up the pastry edges and crimp them together along the top, making sure they are tightly sealed.

4 Transfer the pasties to a baking sheet, brush beaten egg all over them and bake in an oven preheated to 180°C/Gas Mark 4 for 25 minutes. Lower the heat to 160°C/Gas Mark 3 and bake for a further 20 minutes, until golden brown.

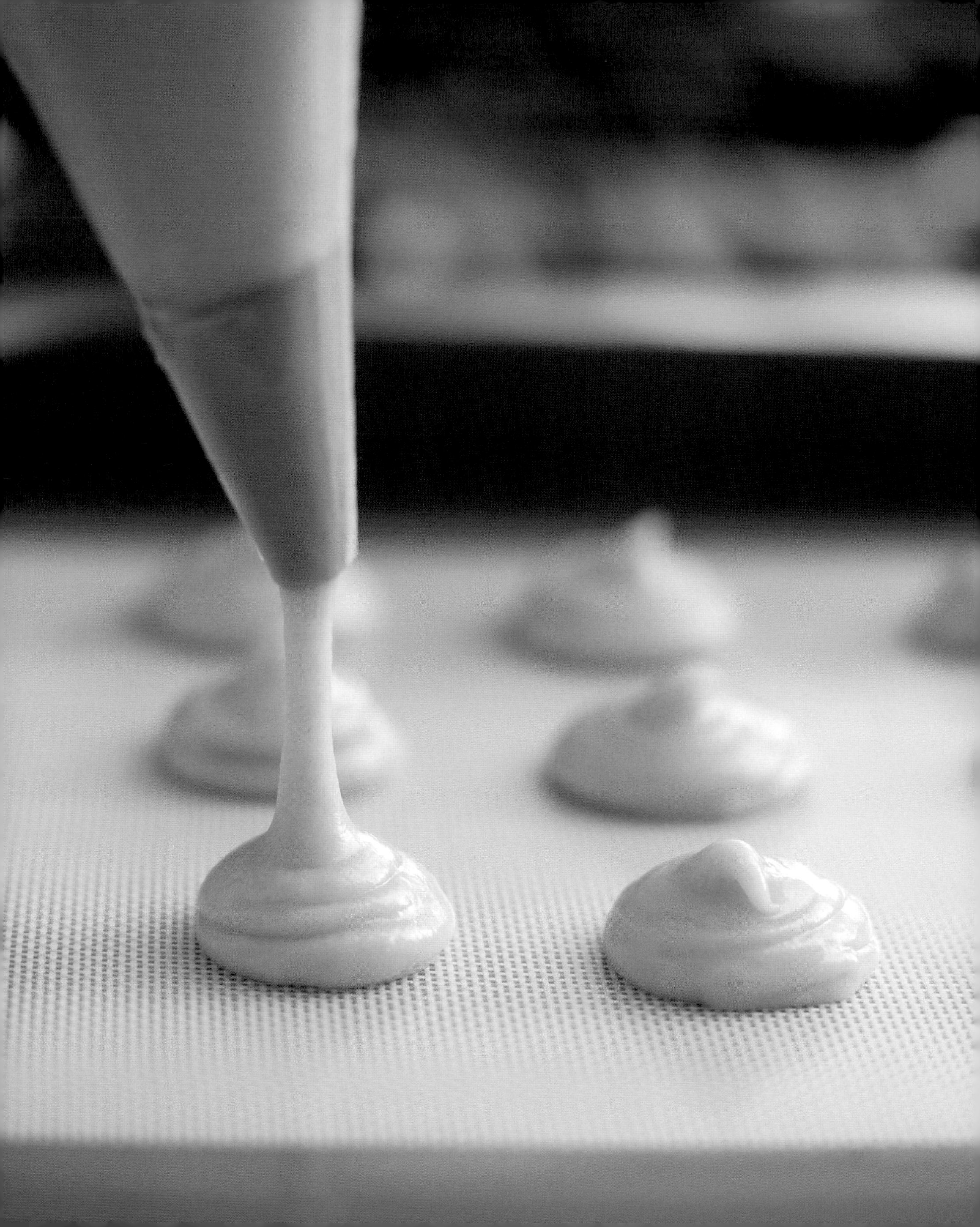

CHOUX PASTRY

Choux pastry is not really like pastry at all.
It is a very thick paste that rises to twice its
size in the oven, thanks to the high egg content,
becoming crisp and golden. The wonderful thing
about choux is that because it has a hollow, airy
centre, you can fill it with anything you like,
sweet or savoury. It is incredibly versatile and
can even be mixed with mashed potato and baked
or fried to make little beignets. Choux pastry
is perhaps best known in chocolate éclairs but
other classic uses include dramatic desserts such
as the French Pièce Montée (see page 128)
and Paris-Brest (see page 126).

Profiteroles with chocolate sauce have never gone out of fashion — quite an homage to choux pastry. I absolutely adore them, but like to make the profiteroles very small. You can make bigger ones, if you prefer.

PROFITEROLES

To make the basic Choux Pastry, follow steps 1 to 4
To make Crème Pâtissière, follow steps 10 to 15

MAKES 500G CHOUX PASTRY
AND 40–50 SMALL PROFITEROLES

200ml water

90g unsalted butter

120g plain flour

4 medium eggs (total weight about 200g in their shells)

FOR THE CRÈME PÂTISSIÈRE:

4 egg yolks

20g plain flour

1 teaspoon cornflour

70g caster sugar

300ml full-fat milk

1 vanilla pod, split open lengthways

200ml double cream

FOR THE CHOCOLATE SAUCE:

100g dark chocolate (60–70% cocoa solids), broken into pieces

120ml water

80 unsalted butter, diced

60g caster sugar

1 Boil the water and butter together, mixing well.

2 Remove from the heat and add all the flour, stirring vigorously. The mixture should thicken and come away clean from the side of the saucepan.

3 Return the saucepan to the heat for a couple of minutes to allow the mixture to dry out, continuing to mix vigorously.

4 Transfer it to a cold bowl, then set aside to cool for 2 minutes.

5 Mix in the eggs one by one. Spoon the mixture into a piping bag fitted with a plain 1cm nozzle.

6 Pipe 40–50 balls the size of small walnuts on to baking parchment-lined baking sheets, spacing them at least 2.5cm apart.

7 Push down any points with a wet finger.

8 Bake in an oven preheated to 200°C/Gas Mark 6 for 20–25 minutes, until golden brown.

9 Then lower the heat to 140°C/Gas Mark 1 and bake for a further 20 minutes, or until dried out. Set aside to cool.

10 To make the crème pâtissière, put the egg yolks, flour, cornflour and sugar in a bowl and whisk with a balloon whisk.

11 Put the milk and vanilla pod into a saucepan and bring to the boil.

12 Pour the milk on to the egg mixture, whisking all the time.

13 Return the mixture to the pan and heat slowly, stirring constantly, until it starts to thicken. Continue heating and stirring for 1–2 minutes.

14 Push the mixture through a sieve into a bowl, discarding the vanilla pod, then cover with cling film and leave until cold.

15 Whip the cream to very soft peaks and fold it into the crème pâtissière. Set aside to cool for 10 minutes.

16 Spoon into a piping bag fitted with a plain 5mm nozzle.

17 To fill the choux buns, make a hole in the bottom of each one with the point of a sharp knife.

18 Insert the piping bag nozzle and squeeze in some crème pâtissière.

19 To make the sauce, put the chocolate in a small, heavy-based pan with the water and heat gently, stirring constantly, until melted.

20 Add the butter and sugar and keep stirring until the butter has melted. Transfer the sauce to a bowl and place in the fridge to cool.

21 To serve, arrange the profiteroles in a pyramid on a large platter or individual plates and pour the sauce over them.

choux variations

Gougères – make the choux pastry as described on page 121, steps 1–4, adding 75g grated strong Cheddar cheese to the final mixture. Pipe the choux mixture into balls, as described on page 121, steps 5–7, and bake in an oven preheated to 180°C/Gas Mark 4 for 20 minutes, until golden brown.

Choux Shapes – make the choux pastry as described on page 121, steps 1–4, then pipe the choux mixture into rings, zigzags or whatever shape you like on the prepared sheets and bake in an oven preheated to 200°C/Gas Mark 6 for 25 minutes. Allow to cool, then dust with sifted icing sugar and serve.

Cheese Fritters – make the choux pastry as described on page 121, steps 1–4, adding 250g grated Cheddar cheese to the final mixture and seasoning well with salt and pepper. Heat a one-third depth of sunflower oil to 190°C in a saucepan, then pipe in the choux pastry, cutting off each piece at the size of a walnut. Cook until golden brown, then lift out with a slotted spoon and drain well on kitchen paper. Serve immediately.

TIPS AND IDEAS

■ When making choux pastry, add the flour all at once, stirring constantly, otherwise it can become lumpy.

■ Make sure you beat in each egg very thoroughly before adding the next. The final egg can be added a little at a time to ensure you have the correct consistency. The mixture should be shiny and just soft enough to fall from the spoon – you may not need quite all the egg.

■ Never add the eggs to the hot saucepan – always transfer the dough to a large, cold bowl and allow it to cool slightly before adding the eggs.

■ If you wish to add cheese to the dough for a savoury pastry, always do so at the end of the making; similarly, if you want to make a sweet dough, add sugar at the end too.

■ Always leave plenty of room between choux pastries because they expand to twice the size in the oven.

■ Make sure the baked choux is dry; if not, keep it in the oven a little longer.

■ Eat choux pastry on the day it is made, or freeze it straight away.

■ If you want to make the crème pâtissière in advance, a good tip is not to include the sugar but to sprinkle it on top at the end – this prevents the crème pâtissière forming a skin as it cools. Simply stir in the sugar before adding the cream.

■ When filling the choux buns, it can be difficult to know when they're full enough. The best thing is to go by weight – the bun should feel noticeably heavier in your hand.

■ If you want to keep the choux buns crisp, fill them no more than an hour before serving.

ECLAIRS

I love these little morsels. The method is exactly the same as for the profiteroles on page 120 but the choux is piped into lengths rather than round buns.

Makes about 18

1 quantity Choux Pastry (see pages 120–121, steps 1–4)

For the filling:

200ml double cream

60g caster sugar

150g Crème Pâtissière (optional, see pages 120–122, steps 10–15)

For the icing:

50ml double cream

150g dark chocolate (60–70% cocoa solids), broken into pieces

1 Spoon the choux mixture into a large piping bag fitted with a plain 1cm nozzle and pipe 10cm lengths of it on to baking parchment-lined baking sheets, spacing them 1.5cm apart. Push down any points with a wet finger.

2 Bake in an oven preheated to 220°C/Gas Mark 7 for 20 minutes, then lower the heat to 140°C/Gas Mark 1 and bake for a further 20 minutes. Set aside to cool.

3 To make the filling, whip the cream and sugar into stiff peaks, then fold the mixture into the crème pâtissière (if using). Spoon into a piping bag fitted with a plain 3mm nozzle.

4 To fill the éclairs, make a hole in the end of each one with the point of a sharp knife, insert the piping bag nozzle and squeeze in some of the filling.

5 To make the icing, put the cream into a pan and bring to the boil. Put the chocolate into a heatproof bowl and pour the hot cream over it. Leave for a minute and then stir gently to melt the chocolate. Remove from the heat and leave to cool until it starts to thicken slightly.

6 Spoon the icing over the top of the éclairs or dip the éclairs in the icing and set aside until cold.

PARIS–BREST

Created in the late nineteenth century to celebrate the Paris to Brest cycling race, this is shaped to resemble a bicycle tyre. I like to serve it with strawberries in the summer.

Serves 6

1 quantity Choux Pastry (see pages 120–121, steps 1–4)

1 egg plus 1 egg yolk, beaten together, for glazing

60g flaked almonds

sifted icing sugar for dusting

For the crème pâtissière buttercream:

4 egg yolks

200g caster sugar

30g cornflour

400ml full-fat milk

70g dark chocolate (60–70% cocoa solids), cut into small pieces

300g soft unsalted butter

100g icing sugar, sifted

1 First make the buttercream. Put the egg yolks, caster sugar and cornflour in a bowl and mix well. Add a little of the milk, mixing until there are no lumps, then pour in the rest of the milk, whisking all the time. Transfer the mixture to a saucepan, bring to a simmer and stir until you have a smooth, thick cream. Remove from the heat, add the chocolate and stir until melted. Transfer to a bowl and set aside until cold.

2 Whisk the butter and icing sugar together in a bowl until soft and smooth. Fold in the cold chocolate mixture, then set aside until needed.

3 Line a baking sheet with baking parchment, place a 20cm saucepan lid on it and draw around it with a pencil. Spoon the choux pastry into a piping bag fitted with a 1cm star nozzle and pipe around the pencilled circle a few times, working from the outside in, until you have a ring 5cm wide. Push down any points with a wet finger. Brush with the beaten eggs, then sprinkle with the almonds.

4 Bake in an oven preheated to 220°C/Gas Mark 7 for 15 minutes, then lower the heat to 140°C/Gas Mark 1 and cook for a further 35–40 minutes, until dried out. Transfer to a wire rack until cold.

5 Cut the choux circle in half horizontally and open it out. Pipe the buttercream on to the lower half of the ring and place the upper half on top. Dust with icing sugar before serving.

PASSION FRUIT FINGERS

This is a lovely alternative way to serve éclairs. Mango purée also works well in the filling. You could cut them open and add raspberries or sliced strawberries, then sandwich together.

Makes 8

1 quantity Choux Pastry (see pages 120–121, steps 1–4)

For the filling:

250ml full-fat milk

3 egg yolks

100g caster sugar

30g plain flour

60ml canned passion fruit purée

150ml double cream

1 tablespoon icing sugar, plus extra, sifted, for dusting

1 Line a baking sheet with baking parchment. Spoon the choux mixture into a large piping bag fitted with a plain 1cm nozzle and pipe eight 15cm lengths on to the prepared sheet, spacing them 1.5cm apart. Push down any points with a wet finger.

2 Bake in an oven preheated to 200°C/Gas Mark 6 for 10 minutes, then lower the heat to 180°C/Gas Mark 4 and bake for a further 15 minutes, until dry inside. Transfer the fingers to a wire rack and make a small incision in the end of each one to release the steam.

3 Put the milk in a pan and bring to the boil. Meanwhile, put the egg yolks and caster sugar in a bowl and whisk until pale. Beat in the flour and boiling milk, then return the mixture to the milk pan and thicken over a low heat, stirring constantly. Add the passion fruit purée and set aside to cool.

4 Whip the cream with the icing sugar into soft peaks and fold into the egg mixture. Spoon into a piping bag fitted with a plain 3mm nozzle and fill the fingers with it via the steam-hole. Dust with icing sugar before serving.

---

choux finger variation

Fruity Choux Buns – pipe 9 tennis ball-sized mounds of choux pastry on to the prepared baking sheets, spacing them at least 3cm apart. Bake in an oven preheated to 200°C/Gas Mark 6 for 25–30 minutes, until golden brown. Transfer to a wire rack until cold, then cut the buns in half. Fill with Chantilly Cream (see Strawberry and Chantilly Cream Swiss Roll, page 78) and add some fruit, such as mango slices, strawberries or raspberries. Cut the 'lid' of each bun in half and insert the 2 semicircles back to back in the cream like butterfly wings. Sprinkle with sifted icing sugar before serving.

PIÈCE MONTÉE

This is easier to tackle than the famous croquembouche and is simply a mountain of profiteroles stuck together with caramel. I think it's equally dramatic and, if you are having a party, it's a wonderful thing to do. Be sure to read the tips for choux pastry on page 124 to ensure success. Also, watch out for the caramel when dipping the buns in it — it can burn your fingers badly.

Serves 12–14

2 quantities Choux Pastry (see pages 120–121, steps 1–4)

2 quantities Crème Pâtissière (see pages 120–122, steps 10–15)

sifted icing sugar for sprinkling

For the caramel:

700g granulated sugar

4 tablespoons water

1 Line 2 baking sheets with baking parchment. Spoon the choux mixture into a piping bag fitted with a plain 1cm nozzle and pipe about 65 balls the size of small walnuts on to the prepared sheets, spacing them at least 2cm apart. Push down any points with a wet finger. Bake in an oven preheated to 200°C/Gas Mark 6 for 15 minutes, then lower the heat to 140°C/Gas Mark 1 for a further 20–25 minutes, until dried out. Transfer to a wire rack until cold. Make another batch of buns in the same way – you need about 130 in total.

2 Using the point of a sharp knife, make a hole in the bottom of each cold bun. Spoon the crème pâtissière into a piping bag fitted with a plain 3mm nozzle and pipe it into the buns.

3 To make the caramel, put the sugar and water into a saucepan over a medium heat and move the mixture from side to side – do not stir – with a wooden spoon. Once the mixture starts to brown, bring to the boil and bubble until it becomes a light caramel colour. Take off heat.

4 If you want to make a 'mountain' of the buns, start with a base circle 22cm in diameter, carefully dipping a corner of each bun into the caramel and sticking them together in graduated circles to make a cone shape. When the cone is complete, re-melt the remaining caramel and sprinkle it evenly over the top. Set aside until the caramel hardens (about 10 minutes), then sprinkle with icing sugar. Serve within 2–3 hours of making.

5 If you want to make a flatter heap of the buns, simply arrange them in graduated circles to fit your serving platter – they do not need to be stuck together – and dribble the caramel all over the heap.

CHEESY HERB PROFITEROLES

Choux pastry makes a wonderfully light vehicle for savoury flavours. These are delicious nibbles to serve with drinks.

Makes 40

100g Gruyère cheese, grated

1 tablespoon finely chopped parsley

2 teaspoons ground cumin

1 teaspoon chilli powder

1 quantity Choux Pastry made with 60g unsalted butter (see pages 120–121, steps 1–4)

1 Add the cheese, parsley, cumin and chilli powder to the basic choux paste and mix well. Spoon the mixture into a large piping bag fitted with a plain 1cm nozzle and pipe walnut-sized balls on to a baking parchment-lined baking sheet, spacing them 2cm apart. Push down any points with a wet finger.

2 Bake in an oven preheated to 200°C/Gas Mark 6 for about 35 minutes. Serve hot.

DAUPHINE POTATOES

Old-fashioned but irresistible — especially with lamb, chicken and other meats. Don't be tempted to add butter to the mashed potato or the mixture will be too soft.

Makes 18–20

1kg potatoes

½ quantity Choux Pastry (see pages 120–121, steps 1–4)

1 egg yolk, beaten

60g plain flour, plus extra for dusting

oil for frying

sea salt and black pepper

1 Peel the potatoes, cut into equal-sized pieces and boil for about 20 minutes, or until soft. Drain well, then transfer to a cold bowl. Add the choux mixture, egg yolk, flour and seasoning and mix well.

2 Place a sheet of greaseproof paper on a baking sheet and dust it with flour. Now flour your hands and make small balls of the potato mixture, each weighing about 30g. Place them on the floured paper and chill for 1 hour.

3 Fill a large saucepan one-third deep with oil and heat it to 170°C. Carefully add 5 or 6 potato balls to the pan and fry until golden brown all over. Remove with a slotted spoon and drain well on kitchen paper. Keep warm while you cook the remaining potato balls, and serve hot. Alternatively, keep the cooked balls in a cool place until needed, then place them on a baking sheet in an oven preheated to 180°C/Gas Mark 4 for about 15 minutes.

PUFF PASTRY

There is nothing to beat homemade puff pastry —
it is infinitely superior to the bought equivalent.
Making it involves a certain amount of technique
but it really isn't difficult; you just need to take
a methodical approach. The sense of pride on
achieving it is so rewarding. One of my favourite
ways to eat puff pastry is in the Chicken and
Potato Pie on page 148, but it's also delicious
in sweet dishes — try it drenched in caramel in
a classic tarte Tatin (see page 132) or cut into
light, crisp fingers and layered with strawberries
and pastry cream for a mille-feuille (page 140).

Apple is traditional, but pear is my favourite version of all: tender pear and sweet caramel are a heavenly combination. Other fruits can work well too, but it's best to go for firm ones with a touch of acidity.

PEAR TARTE TATIN

To make the basic Puff Pastry, follow steps 1 to 19
To make the basic Tarte Tatin, follow steps 20 to 30

MAKES 2KG PUFF PASTRY AND THE TART
SERVES 4

juice of 1 lemon

3 ripe pears

250g caster sugar

2 tablespoons Poire William liqueur, warmed

150g unsalted butter, cut into small pieces

FOR THE PUFF PASTRY:

500g plain flour, plus extra for dusting

680g unsalted butter, cut into small pieces

250g strong white flour

225ml water

15g sea salt

1 First make a butterball for the pastry. Put half the plain flour into a bowl with 600g of the butter.

2 Mix together without beating until you can form a ball from the mixture. Cover with cling film and then chill for 2 hours.

3 Put the remaining plain flour and strong flour into a bowl, make a well and add the water, remaining butter and salt.

4 Mix well until it forms a smooth dough. It should have the same consistency as the chilled butterball, so do not put too much pressure on it.

5 Cover with cling film and chill for 2 hours.

6 When ready to use, place the dough on a floured work surface.

7 Press down a little with the palm of one hand, resting the other on top and push (not stretch) the dough until it forms a circle about 4cm thick.

8 Start rolling the dough into the shape of a four-leaf clover, leaving it slightly domed in the middle.

9 The leaves tend to come back on themselves, so roll again until they stay put.

10 Place the butterball in the middle of the dough and fold the first leaf over it without stretching, and brushing off any excess flour.

11 Bring the next leaf up and over, brushing off the flour again, and repeat with the other 2 leaves. Make sure the corners are well sealed.

12 Push down as before with the palm of your hand, again without stretching, to make a circle about 4cm thick.

13 Roll the pastry into a strip about 38cm long and 3mm thick. Fold it into 3, then turn the dough through 90 degrees to the open end.

14 Now roll again to the same size, keeping the pastry as even as possible. Fold again into 3, then turn again through 90 degrees to the open end.

15 Cover with cling film and chill for 25 minutes to allow the gluten to rest.

16 Roll out the chilled dough as before, folding it into 3 and turning it through 90 degrees to the open end.

17 Repeat once again, then cover and chill for another 25 minutes.

18 Roll and repeat the final 2 turns. This now gives it 6 turns. Cover with cling film and chill for at least 4 hours.

19 Trim off the sides, wrap the offcuts in cling film and freeze. These bits are handy for making Palmiers (see page 142) or using as pie toppings.

20 Fill a mixing bowl with cold water and add the lemon juice. Peel the pears, cut them in half lengthways and carefully remove the cores.

21 Place the pear halves in the prepared water.

22 Put the sugar in a heavy-based saucepan over a low heat until it melts.

23 As the sugar starts to caramelise, gently move it around without stirring, lowering the heat a little if necessary.

24 When the sugar has completely caramelised, take it off the heat, add the liqueur and stir until smooth.

PUFF PASTRY

25 Return to the heat, add the butter and simmer, stirring constantly, until the mixture starts to thicken.

26 Pour into a shallow non-stick baking tin about 18cm in diameter.

27 Drain the pears and arrange flat-side up in a neat pattern on top of the caramel, to appear domed-side up once the tart is turned over.

28 On a lightly floured work surface, roll out the pastry so that it is 2cm wider than the baking tin. Cut the pastry into a rough circle and place it over the pears

29 Tuck the pastry around the edges. Bake in an oven preheated to 200°C/ Gas Mark 6 for about 45 minutes, until golden.

30 Set aside to cool for 5 minutes before turning it out on to a plate, taking care as the caramel will still be warm.

TIPS AND IDEAS

■ The trick to making puff pastry is to work as quickly as possible so that everything stays cool. It's not something to do in a hot kitchen. Make sure all the ingredients except the butter are cold before you start. The flour can be put in the fridge and the water should be ice cold.

■ The pastry dough needs to be the same consistency as the butterball, otherwise it will tear and the butter will come through.

■ If the butter does start to show through, sprinkle a little flour on it. As long as everything is cold, it will be fine.

■ I like to make double this amount of pastry and store a batch in the freezer. It can be frozen for up to 2 months, but it won't keep for more than 2 days in the fridge, becoming grey and grainy.

■ Puff pastry should be cooked until golden and crisp rather than soft. The only exception to the rule is the Apple and Raisin, Pistachio and Cinnamon Log on page 138.

■ In recipes where you need to glaze the pastry, don't brush the glaze beyond the pastry edges on to the tin or baking sheet, or it will prevent it rising.

■ To give a crisp topping to sweet pies, glaze the pastry with egg and then sprinkle sugar over the top.

■ For the tarte Tatin, make sure you tuck the edges of the pastry in firmly when you put it over the fruit, otherwise it won't look so pretty when it is turned out.

tarte Tatin variations

Quick Puff Pastry – put 500g plain flour into a bowl, add 500g unsalted butter, cut into small pieces, and rub together until the mixture resembles breadcrumbs. Add 250ml iced water and 2 teaspoons salt, and mix until a dough forms. On a lightly floured work surface, roll into a rectangle, fold into 3 and turn through 90 degrees. Repeat this process twice more, then cover with cling film and chill until required.

Mango and Lavender Tarte Tatin – follow the main recipe on pages 132–135, using 3 slightly underripe mangoes instead of the pears. Cut each mango in half lengthways, remove the peel and stone, then cut each half into 3 strips. Omit steps 20 and 21, and add 1 tablespoon lavender flowers instead of the Poire William liqueur in step 24.

Individual Pineapple Tarte Tatins – make the puff pastry as described on pages 132–134, steps 1–19. Generously butter four 10cm tart tins and line each one with a circle of baking parchment. Peel half a fresh pineapple and cut into 4 slices 1cm thick. Remove the core with a small cutter. Make the caramel as on page 134, steps 22–25, adding the seeds from 8 cardamom pods instead of the pear liqueur. Pour 2 tablespoons of caramel into each prepared tin and place a circle of pineapple in it. Roll out the puff pastry and cut out four 12cm circles. Place one on top of each pineapple slice, tucking it down the sides as on page 135, step 29. Bake at 200°C/Gas Mark 6 for 15 minutes, then at 180°C/Gas Mark 4 for a further 10 minutes.

BANANA AND RUM PASTRIES

These gently spiced little pasties are lovely served warm with cream, custard or ice cream for pudding.

Makes 24

3 ripe bananas, cut into 2cm slices

20g unsalted butter, plus extra for greasing

1 tablespoon caster sugar

1 tablespoon honey

1 teaspoon ground allspice

zest of 1 lemon

1 tablespoon rum

icing sugar for dusting

½ quantity Puff Pastry (see pages 132–134, steps 1–19)

1 egg, beaten, for glazing

1 Place the bananas in a saucepan with the butter, sugar, honey, allspice, lemon zest and rum and cook over a medium heat for about 5 minutes, until syrupy. Set aside to cool.

2 Dust a work surface with icing sugar and roll out the pastry as thinly as possible. Using a 7cm cutter, stamp out 24 circles.

3 Put a heaped teaspoonful of the banana filling on one half of each circle and fold the pastry over to form semicircles. Pinch the edges with your fingers, then roll inwards to make a festoon effect.

4 Place the puffs on a silicone baking mat or buttered baking sheet and brush with beaten egg. Bake in an oven preheated to 190°C/Gas Mark 5 for about 20 minutes, until puffed and golden.

PALMIERS

Save up all your precious puff pastry trimmings in the freezer and then use them to make these delicious crisp, sugared wafers.

Makes 20 palmiers

icing sugar for dusting

300g Puff Pastry (see pages 132–134, steps 1–19)

flour for dusting

1 Sift some icing sugar on to a work surface and roll the pastry into a rectangle about 30 x 25cm. Now tightly roll one short side into the centre, and repeat with the opposite side. Cover with cling film and chill for 2 hours.

2 Place the rolled pastry on a chopping board and cut into slices 5mm thick. Place them on a baking sheet lined with baking parchment, spacing them about 2.5cm apart. Bake in an oven preheated to 200°C/Gas Mark 6 for 20–25 minutes, until golden. Cool on a wire rack.

palmier variations

Sweet Puff Pastry Thins – dust a work surface with sifted icing sugar and roll out 250g Puff Pastry (see pages 132–134, steps 1–19) into a rectangle about 2cm thick. Roll it up lengthways into a log, wrap in cling film and chill for 30 minutes. Slice into 3cm pieces, then roll each piece into a rectangle about 13 x 6cm. (For a more precise shape, cut a template from an old ice cream container, place it on the pastry and cut around it.) Bake just a few at a time on a non-stick baking sheet in an oven preheated to 180°C/Gas Mark 4 for about 15 minutes, or until golden. Meanwhile, fill a heavy pan with ice to make it cold. Transfer the baked pastries to a cold metal surface, then press the ice-cold pan over them, one at a time, for just a few seconds to caramelise the sugar. Cool on a wire rack. These thins are lovely layered with fruit and cream, or served alongside ice cream.

Cheesy Palmiers – roll out 250g Puff Pastry as described above. Brush with beaten egg and scatter 80g finely grated Cheddar cheese over the surface. Sprinkle with salt, pepper and smoked paprika. Roll up, slice and bake as described above.

ANCHOVY STRAWS

I prefer to use marinated anchovies for these rather than the ones in oil, which I find too strong. This recipe makes enough for a party.

Makes 50

250g Puff Pastry (see pages 132–134, steps 1–19)

flour for dusting

75g marinated anchovy fillets, drained and halved lengthways

cayenne pepper

1 Place one half of the pastry on a lightly floured work surface and roll it into a rectangle about 30 x 25cm. Put a line of anchovies parallel to the long edge of the pastry, then place more lines underneath, spacing them about 1.5cm apart.

2 Roll out the other half of the pastry to the same size as the first and place it on top. Roll the 2 sheets together until wafer thin. Place on a floured tray or board and put into the freezer for about 1 hour to become firm.

3 Working quickly, cut the chilled pastry into very thin strips about 3mm wide. Arrange the pastry strips on a non-stick baking sheet and bake in an oven preheated to 190°C/Gas Mark 5 for 10–12 minutes, until golden brown.

---

anchovy straw variations

Chilli Straws – follow the method above, but make lines of dried chilli flakes or powder instead of anchovies.

Cheese Straws – follow the method above, making lines of freshly grated Parmesan cheese instead of anchovies.

LEEK, TOMATO AND GOATS' CHEESE TART

I love goat's cheese with anything, but it goes particularly well with leeks and tomato.

Serves 4

flour for dusting

1 quantity Puff Pastry (see pages 132–134, steps 1–19)

1 egg, beaten, for glazing

For the filling:

300g leeks, finely sliced

80g unsalted butter, plus extra for greasing

100g goats' cheese, crumbled

3 rounded tablespoons chopped chives

150g tomatoes, finely sliced

50g Cheddar cheese, grated

sea salt and black pepper

1 On a lightly floured work surface, roll the pastry into a circle 25cm wide and 2mm thick. Cut a circle 23cm diameter, then cut another circle inside it, this time 20cm wide. This will give you a neat border of pastry 3cm wide. Brush the perimeter of the inner circle with beaten egg, then place the 3cm border on it, cutting it to fit without overlapping. Place on a buttered baking sheet, brush the raised edge with beaten egg and bake in an oven preheated to 190°C/Gas Mark 5 for 15–20 minutes, until golden.

2 Meanwhile, put the leeks and butter into a large frying pan and cook gently for 20 minutes without browning. Season with salt and pepper and set aside until cold.

3 Add the goats' cheese and chives to the leek mixture, season well, then put the mixture into the pastry case. Arrange the tomato slices neatly on top and sprinkle with the Cheddar. Bake in an oven preheated to 180°C/Gas Mark 4 for 20 minutes, or until the cheese has melted and is light golden brown.

PUFF PASTRY CANAPÉS

These little pinwheels always go down well at parties. They can be assembled in advance, then sliced and baked at the last minute and served hot from the oven. I have given two savoury fillings and a sweet one here. You can make up your own fillings, but be sure to choose fairly strong flavours so that the taste comes through.

Makes 48 of each filling

flour for dusting

750g Puff Pastry (see pages 132–134, steps 1–19)

unsalted butter for greasing

For the tapenade filling:

100g full-fat cream cheese

4 tablespoons tapenade

4 slices of Parma ham

For the cheese and anchovy filling:

50g Cheddar cheese, grated

50g Parmesan cheese, freshly grated

½ teaspoon cayenne pepper

150g anchovy fillets in oil, drained and chopped

For the hazelnut filling:

125g hazelnuts, finely chopped

25g fresh white breadcrumbs

35g caster sugar

2 tablespoons rum

1 On a lightly floured work surface, roll the pastry into a large rectangle about 40 x 30cm and 2.5mm thick. Place on a floured baking sheet and chill for 30 minutes.

2 Meanwhile make the fillings. Put the cream cheese and tapenade into a bowl and mix well. Cover with cling film and leave in the fridge until needed. Combine the ingredients for the other 2 fillings in separate bowls, then cover and leave in the fridge until needed.

3 Cut the chilled pastry into 3 equal pieces, each one measuring 40 x 10cm. Spread half the cream cheese mixture on one strip of pastry, lay the Parma ham on top and cover with remaining cream cheese filling. Roll up tightly from the narrow end, wrap in cling film and place in the freezer for 30 minutes.

4 Spread the other fillings on the remaining strips of pastry and roll up as before. Wrap in cling film and place in the freezer for 30 minutes.

5 Cut the chilled pastry rolls into slices 6mm thick and place them on buttered baking sheets, spacing the canapés 1cm apart. Bake in an oven preheated to 180°C/Gas Mark 4 for about 15 minutes, until golden.

PUFF PASTRY OVER CRAB BISQUE

I first ate this 30 years ago and it was one of the most delicious starters I've ever had. I've always wanted to recreate it, so was very happy to be able to include it here. Make sure the bisque is velvety smooth — it really does need to be pushed through a sieve to get the correct texture.

Serves 8–10

2 large cooked crabs

4 tablespoons olive oil

1 small fennel bulb, chopped

1 large onion, chopped

1 leek, chopped

1 carrot, chopped

4 garlic cloves, chopped

½ bottle of dry white wine

2¾ litres fish stock

25g tomatoes, quartered

2 sprigs of thyme

1 potato, chopped into small dice

250g tomato purée

500g raw prawns in their shells (optional)

150ml double cream

beurre manié (40g butter mixed with 40g flour)

flour for dusting

1 quantity Puff Pastry (see pages 132–134, steps 1–19)

1 egg, beaten, for glazing

sea salt and cayenne pepper

1 Take the crabmeat from the shells, keeping the brown meat separate and reserving the white for use in another dish. Put the shells in a roasting tin with 3 tablespoons of the olive oil and place over a high heat until fragrant. Add the fennel, onion, leek, carrot and garlic and cook gently until soft. Pour in the wine, bring to the boil, then simmer for a minute or two. Add the fish stock, tomatoes and thyme, and simmer for 25 minutes. Strain into a large bowl, pressing the contents thoroughly to extract maximum flavour.

2 Return the liquid to the pan, add the brown crabmeat and potato and simmer for a further 10 minutes, adding the prawns (if using) for the last minute. Using a blender or food processor, liquidise the soup and rub it through a fine sieve. If you like, you can strain it again through an even finer sieve to make it like velvet.

3 Return the soup to the pan and bring to a simmer. Add the cream, then whisk in the beurre manié bit by bit until the soup reaches a rich consistency. Season with salt and cayenne pepper, then set aside until cold.

4 Ladle the bisque into ovenproof soup bowls, filling them three-quarters full. Roll out the pastry on a lightly floured work surface and cut 1cm strips long enough to fit around the rim of the bowls. Press them in place and brush with beaten egg. Now cut out pastry circles a little larger than the bowls. Place them over the egged rim, allowing them to overhang a little as they will shrink when baked. Cut a steam-hole in the centre, brush with beaten egg, then bake in an oven preheated to 200°C/Gas Mark 6 for 20 minutes.

CHICKEN IN PUFF PASTRY

Here a simple chicken mousse is layered with slices of chicken breast and sandwiched between spinach leaves and puff pastry to make 4 individual pies. They are baked and served with a tarragon sauce. There's quite a lot of work involved, but the pies can be assembled well in advance and kept in the fridge until you are ready to bake them.

Serves 4

4 small skinless, boneless chicken breasts

1 egg white

a pinch of cayenne pepper

a pinch of freshly grated nutmeg

150ml double cream

8 large spinach leaves

600g Puff Pastry (see pages 132–134, steps 1–19)

flour for dusting

2 egg yolks, lightly beaten, for glazing

sea salt and black pepper

For the sauce:

30g unsalted butter, plus extra for greasing

1 rasher of bacon, chopped

1 leek, chopped

a few tarragon leaves

6 medium mushrooms, chopped

250ml white wine

300ml chicken stock

150ml vermouth

120ml double cream

1 Put 2 of the chicken breasts into a food processor and whiz until smooth. Add the egg white, process until combined, then season well with salt and pepper, and the cayenne and nutmeg. Transfer to a bowl and slowly whisk in the cream. You should now have quite a thick mousse.

2 Blanch the spinach in simmering water for 30 seconds, drain and refresh under running cold water, then place on a tea towel to dry.

3 Place the pastry on a lightly floured work surface and roll out to a thickness of 2–3mm. Cut 4 circles 9cm in diameter, and another 4 circles 14cm in diameter. Brush beaten egg yolk over the small circles and place a spinach leaf on each one, leaving a 1cm margin of pastry all around it, then place a rounded teaspoonful of mousse on top.

4 Slice the 2 remaining chicken breasts in half horizontally and then across. Lay a chicken slice over the mousse, top with another spoonful of mousse, another slice of chicken and another spoonful of mousse. Place a spinach leaf on top, cover with a large pastry circle and press around the edges to seal. Chill for 1 hour to firm up.

5 Trim the edges of each pie to neaten, then use the tip of a very sharp knife to cut a steam-hole in the top. Brush beaten egg yolk over the surface of the pies, then place on a buttered baking sheet and bake in an oven preheated to 200°C/Gas Mark 6 for 30 minutes.

6 To make the sauce, melt the butter in a frying pan, add the bacon, leek and tarragon and cook until soft. Stir in the mushrooms, then add the wine and reduce to one-third. Add the stock and reduce to one-third, then do the same with the vermouth. Finally, add the cream and seasoning. Serve the sauce with the pies.

CHICKEN AND POTATO PIE

This is my famous chicken and potato pie, which I've made countless times. It's my family's favourite dish and if I had to choose a last meal this would probably be it. The trick is to make sure the potato is very well seasoned, otherwise it can be bland. It's a rustic dish, to be placed in the centre of the table so that everyone can help themselves. I once cooked 36 of these pies for a friend's wedding, one on each table.

Serves 6–8

750g potatoes, thinly sliced

130g unsalted butter, plus extra for greasing

3 shallots, finely chopped

2 tablespoons tarragon leaves

2 tablespoons chopped chives

4 large skinless, boneless chicken breasts, cut into thin strips

800g Puff Pastry (see pages 132–134, steps 1–19)

flour for dusting

2 egg yolks, lightly beaten, for glazing

240ml double cream

sea salt and black pepper

1 Put the potatoes and half the butter into a pan and heat gently, turning from time to time, until they are just tender but not brown. Transfer them to a large bowl and set aside to cool.

2 Meanwhile, soften the shallots in the remaining butter. Add the herbs and chicken, turning the mixture over a steady heat for a few minutes until the meat is partially cooked. Add to the bowl of potatoes, mix carefully and season well with salt and pepper. Set aside to cool.

3 Place half the pastry on a lightly floured work surface and roll it into a circle about 30cm wide. Transfer it to a lightly buttered baking sheet. Brush the perimeter of the pastry with beaten egg yolk, then pile the chicken mixture in the middle. Roll the remaining pastry into a circle about 36cm wide and place it over the filling, sealing and crimping the edges. Cut a circle about 10cm wide in the top, but leave it in place: this will act as a lid. Brush the whole surface with the remaining egg yolk. Bake in an oven preheated to 180°C/Gas Mark 4 for about 50 minutes, checking that it's not browning too much, in which case lower the heat slightly.

4 When the pie is ready, heat the cream until boiling, then season with salt and pepper. Carefully remove the small pastry lid from the pie and pour in the cream, lifting the mixture gently to allow it to circulate. Put the lid back on and return the pie to the oven for 10 minutes.

VENISON EN CROÛTE WITH RED WINE AND PORT SAUCE

When venison is in season, this makes a lovely alternative to the more traditional beef en croûte. Venison is a wonderfully versatile meat, but it's important to serve it good and rare.

Serves 6–8

1 tablespoon oil, plus extra for greasing

600g loin of venison, well trimmed

550g Puff Pastry (see pages 132–134, steps 1–19)

flour for dusting

250g cooked spinach, squeezed to remove excess water

For the stuffing:

100g chicken livers, picked over and chopped, or chicken liver pâté

60g unsalted butter

2 shallots, very finely chopped

2 garlic cloves, finely chopped

200g wild mushrooms, finely chopped

2 teaspoons thyme leaves

50g fresh white breadcrumbs

sea salt and black pepper

For the sauce:

½ leek, finely chopped

2 shallots, finely chopped

60g unsalted butter

1 rasher of bacon, chopped

½ bottle of red wine

3 tablespoons redcurrant jelly

400ml game or venison stock

200ml veal jus

300ml port

1 First make the stuffing. If using fresh chicken livers, cook them gently in half the butter with the shallots and garlic, until they are pink. When cooked, process or chop the mixture finely. If using pâté, cook just the shallots and garlic in half the butter, then add the pâté to them. In a separate pan, soften the mushrooms with the thyme in the remaining butter, then drain well in a sieve. When both mixtures are cool, mix them together with the breadcrumbs and season well.

2 Heat the oil in a pan and sear the venison all over. Set aside to cool.

3 Roll out the pastry on a lightly floured work surface until it is large enough to enclose the meat; it should be thin but still supple. Arrange the spinach along the middle, then spoon half the stuffing over it. Sit the venison on top and cover it with the rest of the stuffing. To make a neat parcel, cut off and discard the 4 corners of the pastry, then fold in the short ends and wrap the long sides over them. Chill for 1 hour to firm up.

4 Place the parcel on a greased baking sheet in an oven preheated to 200°C/Gas Mark 6 for 20 minutes, then lower the heat to 180°C/Gas Mark 4 and bake for a further 5 minutes. At the change, it is useful to test the meat with a probe to ensure it remains rare – the temperature should not register above 45°C.

5 To make the sauce, soften the leek and shallots in half the butter along with the bacon. Add the wine and redcurrant jelly and simmer until reduced to a syrup. Pour in the stock and cook until reduced by half. Finally, add the veal jus and port, reducing it until slightly thicker. Stir in the remaining butter, season the sauce to your taste and strain it through a sieve. Serve with the venison.

BAKED MEAT SAMOSAS

These are not traditional samosas. Instead they are made with puff pastry and are baked to make delicious pasties, substantial enough to serve as a meal. For a traditional version, you could use the samosa pastry in the box below and deep-fry them instead.

Makes 18

1 medium onion, finely chopped

2 tablespoons olive oil, plus extra for greasing

300g lean lamb, minced twice

1 tablespoon chopped parsley

1 teaspoon ground cinnamon

1 teaspoon ground allspice

1 tablespoon finely chopped raisins

500g Puff Pastry (see page s 132–134, steps 1–19)

flour for dusting

1 egg, beaten, for glazing

sea salt and black pepper

baked meat samosas variation

Traditional Samosa Pastry – sift 400g plain flour and 1 teaspoon salt into a large mixing bowl. Add 100ml vegetable oil and rub into the dry ingredients. Gradually add 200ml lukewarm water and mix to form a firm, smooth dough. On a lightly floured work surface, shape the dough into a log, cover with cling film and chill for 30 minutes. Samosas made with this pastry need to be deep-fried instead of baked. To deep-fry, heat a deep pan one-third full of vegetable oil until it reaches 190°C. Cook a few samosas at a time for about 5 minutes, until golden all over, turning them once during cooking. Using a slotted spoon, transfer to kitchen paper and drain. Serve straight away or place on a wire rack to cool.

1 Fry the onion in the olive oil until soft, then add the lamb and brown it all over. Cover and cook gently for 20 minutes, then add the parsley, spices, raisins and seasoning. Set aside to cool.

2 Divide the pastry into 9 equal pieces and roll each one into a ball. On a lightly floured work surface, roll each of these into a circle about 18cm across and cut the circles in half. Brush the edges of each semicircle with beaten egg and put a tablespoon of filling in the middle. Fold one side of the pastry over the filling and press around the edges to seal in a triangular shape.

3 Place the pastry on a lightly floured work surface and roll out to a thickness of 3mm. Cut into eighteen 8cm squares. Put a tablespoon of the filling in one corner of each square, brush beaten egg around the edges, then fold the opposite pastry corner over the filling and press around the edges to seal in a triangular shape. Brush the top with egg and place on a greased baking sheet. Bake in an oven preheated to 200°C/Gas Mark 6 for 15 minutes. Serve straight away or place on a wire rack to cool.

BAKED VEGETABLE SAMOSAS

I love to serve these spicy samosas for lunch when I have vegetarian guests. They are perfect accompanied by a simple green salad.

Makes 18

400g potatoes

3 tablespoons rapeseed oil, plus extra for greasing

1 teaspoon cumin seeds, crushed

200g onions, finely sliced

2 garlic cloves, finely chopped

1 red chilli, very finely sliced

1 green chilli, very finely sliced

1 teaspoon garam masala

200g frozen peas, cooked

1 teaspoon sea salt

zest of 1 lemon

3 tablespoons coriander leaves

450g Puff Pastry (see pages 132–134, steps 1–19)

flour for dusting

1 egg, beaten, for glazing

1 Cook the potatoes in boiling salted water until just done. Drain well, then cut into 5mm dice.

2 Put 2 tablespoons of the oil in a non-stick frying pan, add the cumin seeds and onions and fry until soft and slightly caramelised. Add the potatoes and garlic with the remaining tablespoon of oil, the chillies and garam masala and cook on a low heat for a further 5 minutes. Add the peas, salt, lemon zest and coriander and cook for another 2 minutes. Set aside to cool for 5 minutes.

3 Place the pastry on a lightly floured work surface and roll out to a thickness of 3mm. Cut into eighteen 8cm squares. Put a tablespoon of the filling in one corner of each square, brush beaten egg around the edges, then fold the opposite pastry corner over the filling and press around the edges to seal in a triangular shape. Brush the top with egg and place on a greased baking sheet. Bake in an oven preheated to 200°C/Gas Mark 6 for 15 minutes. Serve straight away or place on a wire rack to cool.

BÖREK

These little morsels originate from Turkey but are popular throughout North Africa and the Middle East. They can be made with filo or puff pastry, with sweet or savoury fillings, and come in various shapes and sizes – sometimes they are simply made in one large dish and cut into squares or diamonds to serve, like baklava. Here I've given 2 options: little pasties filled with spinach and Gruyère, and triangles with a feta and herb filling.

Makes 50

½ quantity Puff Pastry (see pages 132–134, steps 1–19)

flour for dusting

oil for greasing

1 egg, beaten, for glazing

For the spinach and Gruyère filling:

500g spinach

15g unsalted butter

150g Gruyère cheese, grated

1 egg, beaten

freshly grated nutmeg

sea salt and black pepper

For the feta filling:

500g feta cheese

2 tablespoons chopped dill

2 tablespoons chopped mint

white pepper

1 First make the spinach filling. Put the spinach and butter in a pan and cook until soft. Drain well. Add the Gruyère and beaten egg with a little nutmeg and pepper. Taste to see if the mixture needs any salt. Set aside to cool.

2 To make the feta filling, combine all the ingredients for it in a bowl and mash well.

3 Place the pastry on a lightly floured work surface and roll out as thinly as possible. Using a 7cm cutter, stamp out circles from one half of the pastry, and cut 7cm squares from the other half.

4 Put a heaped teaspoonful of the spinach filling on one half of each circle, brush beaten egg around the edges, then fold the pastry over to form semicircles. Pinch the edges with your fingers and roll to make a festoon effect.

5 Put a heaped teaspoonful of the feta filling near one corner of each square, brush beaten egg around the edges, then fold the opposite pastry corner over the filling and pinch around the edges to seal in a triangular shape. Do make sure they are well sealed, otherwise the parcels can burst during cooking.

6 Put all the börek on a greased baking sheet and brush with beaten egg. Bake in an oven preheated to 190°C/Gas Mark 5 for about 20 minutes, until golden. Serve hot.

STEAMED PUDDINGS

Steamed puddings are pure comfort food. Putting one in the middle of the table brings a smile to everyone's face. A steamed pudding is basically just a sponge cake mixture that has been cooked on the hob, resting above or half in a pan of simmering water, rather than baked. The texture is quite different from a baked cake, but it should be lovely and light. Suet puddings, of course, tend to be sturdier, and can be savoury as well as sweet. Uniquely British, they are perfect winter warmers and often have endearingly eccentric names, such as the famous Spotted Dick (see page 160).

I love homemade marmalade and it really does make the best steamed pudding. You could also use golden syrup here to make a treacle sponge pudding. Serve with custard, cream or ice cream.

MARMALADE STEAMED SPONGE PUDDING

To make the basic Sponge Pudding mixture, follow steps 1 to 3
To cover and steam a pudding, follow steps 4 to 8

SERVES 4–6

120g soft unsalted butter, plus extra for greasing

120g caster sugar

2 eggs

50ml full-fat milk

120g plain flour

2 teaspoons baking powder

zest of 2 lemons

4 rounded tablespoons marmalade

1 Put the butter and sugar in a bowl and cream together until pale. Mix in the eggs, add the milk, then fold in the flour, baking powder and lemon zest.

2 Put the marmalade in the bottom of a buttered 1 litre pudding basin.

3 Spoon in the pudding mixture so that the bowl is three-quarters full.

4 Cover with buttered greaseproof paper and foil (both pleated in the middle to allow for expansion).

5 Tie in place with string, making a looped handle across the top so that the pudding can be easily lifted in and out of the pan.

6 Prepare a steamer – this could just be a pan of boiling water with a trivet or jam jar lid in the bottom.

7 Place the pudding in the steamer, cover and cook over a gentle heat for 2 hours.

8 Check occasionally to ensure the water is always three-quarters of the way up the bowl. When ready, carefully remove the pudding from the pan and peel off the foil and paper.

9 Invert the pudding on to a plate and serve hot.

TIPS AND IDEAS

■ The more you cream the butter and sugar together, the lighter the sponge will be.

■ To stop the mixture curdling when you add the eggs, include a spoonful of the flour with the last addition of egg.

■ Pretty much any flavour can be used in steamed puddings. Try a good compote, such as rhubarb, strawberry or raspberry, or some lemon curd.

■ Only fill the pudding basin three-quarters full, to allow room for the mixture to rise. The reason for making a pleat in the centre of the paper and foil is in case the pudding rises above the top of the dish.

■ I like to cover the basin in the traditional way with paper and foil, but you can buy plastic basins now with snap-on lids, which save a little time and are easy to use.

■ If your pudding rises too high, just cut the top flat so that it sits well when you turn it out on to a plate.

■ When inverting the pudding on to the plate, the marmalade will be red hot, so be very careful.

■ If necessary, you can allow the pudding to cool and then steam it again for 10 minutes or so to reheat it.

■ For an even more flavoursome pudding, heat up a few extra tablespoons of marmalade with a tablespoon of water and pour them over the pudding after turning it out.

steamed sponge pudding variations

Mini Marmalade Puddings – make the sponge pudding mixture as on pages 156–57, steps 1–3. Put a teaspoonful of marmalade in the bottom of 6 buttered 150g pudding basins and pour in the pudding mixture. Cover and steam as on page 157, steps 4–8, for 1 hour.

Lemon Curd Sponge Pudding – make the sponge pudding mixture as on page 157, steps 1–3, but substitute grated orange zest for the lemon in step 1, and lemon curd for the marmalade in step 2. Cover and steam the puddings as before.

Ginger Sponge Pudding – add 2 finely diced balls of stem ginger and 2 tablespoons stem ginger syrup to the sponge pudding mixture at the end of step 1 on page 157. Continue with the main recipe as before.

Chocolate Sponge Pudding – substitute 50g sifted cocoa powder for 50g of the flour in step 1 on page 157. Continue with the main recipe as before.

Glacé Fruit Sponge Pudding – dust 100g glacé fruit in flour and fold it through the sponge pudding mixture at the end of step 1 on page 157. Continue with the main recipe as before.

Eve's Pudding – place 100g raspberry jam in the bottom of a buttered gratin dish. Cover with 300g cold, thick apple purée and spread the sponge pudding mixture, made as on page 157, steps 1–3, over the top. Place the dish in a roasting tin and pour enough boiling water around it to come halfway up the sides. Bake in an oven preheated to 180°C/Gas Mark 4 for 20–25 minutes.

SPOTTED DICK

Anyone of a certain age will associate this with school dinners – it certainly always reminds me of my schooldays. It's a very old-fashioned recipe but delicious when done properly. Traditionally served with custard, it's equally good with cream.

Serves 6

115g small raisins

finely grated zest and juice of 2 lemons

350g plain flour

1 tablespoon baking powder

140g shredded suet

80g caster sugar

30g unsalted butter, plus extra for greasing

180ml full-fat milk

1 Place the raisins and lemon juice and zest in a bowl and set aside to soak for at least 15 minutes.

2 Combine the flour, baking powder, suet and sugar in a large bowl and mix well. Melt the butter and allow to cool until lukewarm, then stir into the flour mixture along with the soaked raisins and enough milk to give a dropping consistency.

3 Butter a 1.5 litre pudding basin, then spoon in the pudding mixture. Cover and steam the pudding (see page 157, steps 4–8) over a gentle heat for about 3 hours, or until cooked through. Turn on to a plate and serve with whipped cream.

CHEAT'S CHRISTMAS PUDDING

This is a very light alternative to Christmas pudding. It contains no fat apart from the suet in the mincemeat but has all the flavour of the original.

Serves 6

450g mincemeat, ideally homemade (if ready-made, drain well)

150g fresh white breadcrumbs

20g plain flour

zest of 1 orange and 1 lemon

1 tablespoon brandy

4 eggs, beaten

unsalted butter for greasing

1 Put the mincemeat into a large bowl with the breadcrumbs, flour, citrus zest, brandy and eggs and mix well.

2 Spoon the mixture into a buttered 1 litre pudding basin, then cover and steam (see page 157, steps 4–8) over a gentle heat for 3 hours, or until cooked through.

CLASSIC CHRISTMAS PUDDING

This pudding is unbelievably good. The recipe makes 2 large puddings, but if you store the extra one in a cool, dry place, it will only improve with keeping and you can serve it the following year — or for any celebration.

Makes two 1.2 litre puddings

4 eggs

100ml rum

150ml fresh orange juice

200ml sweet wine

1 tablespoon treacle

140g self-raising flour

225g shredded suet

200g fresh white breadcrumbs

2 teaspoons ground cinnamon

2 teaspoons ground allspice

400g soft dark brown sugar

200g coarsely grated apple

300g raisins

300g currants

100g flaked almonds

250g sultanas

100g candied mixed peel

100g grated carrot

unsalted butter for greasing

1 Put the eggs, rum, orange juice, wine and treacle in a bowl and whisk together.

2 Put all the other ingredients in a very large bowl and stir well. Add the egg mixture and stir again. Cover with cling film and chill overnight.

3 The next day, divide the chilled mixture between 2 buttered 1.2 litre pudding basins. Cover and steam (see page 157, steps 4–8) over a gentle heat for 4 hours. Set aside until cold, then re-wrap the puddings in fresh greaseproof paper and foil. Store in a cool place (not the fridge) for at least 2 months, but the puddings will keep improving for a year or more.

4 To serve, steam for a further 2 hours.

Christmas Pudding accompaniments

Brandy Butter – place 200g unsalted butter in a bowl and allow it to soften to room temperature. Sift in 150g icing sugar and beat well. Whisk in 3 tablespoons brandy a little at a time until smooth. Extra brandy can be added if you prefer a stronger flavour. Orange zest is a nice addition, and orange juice may be used instead of alcohol if you like.

Rum Chantilly Cream – whisk 250ml double cream with 50g sifted icing sugar until the mixture forms soft peaks. Whisk in 3 tablespoons rum, then cover and chill until required.

This is classic pub fare and so warming. For a Steak and Oyster Pudding, replace the ale with 250ml red wine, use 600ml beef stock and add 8 oysters to the cooked steak mixture.

STEAK AND ALE PUDDING

To make the basic Suet Pastry, follow steps 8 to 9

SERVES 4–6

50g plain flour

800g chuck steak, cut into 2cm dice

60ml oil

60g unsalted butter, plus extra for greasing

3 medium onions, sliced

300ml beef stock

450ml brown ale

200g button mushrooms, cut in half if quite large

1 tablespoon water

2 teaspoons thyme leaves

2 bay leaves

sea salt and black pepper

FOR THE SUET PASTRY:

350g self-raising flour, plus extra for dusting

½ teaspoon bicarbonate of soda

180g shredded suet

½ teaspoon salt

220ml water

1 Put the flour into a large bowl, season with salt and pepper, then toss the beef in it.

2 Heat the oil and half the butter in a frying pan, brown the steak in batches (if necessary) and transfer to a casserole dish.

3 Melt the remaining butter in the pan and fry the onions for a couple of minutes. Add them to the beef along with the stock and ale.

4 Cook the mushrooms in the frying pan with the water. Drain well and add to the casserole dish.

5 Stir in the thyme and bay leaves.

6 Cover and place in an oven preheated to 180°C/Gas Mark 4 for 1½ hours, until the meat is just cooked but still firm, stirring occasionally.

7 Separate the meat from the gravy by straining through a sieve over a saucepan. Set the meat aside to cool to room temperature. Heat the gravy over a low heat until it has reduced.

8 When the filling has cooled, make the pastry. Put the flour and bicarbonate of soda into a large bowl, add the suet and mix well.

9 Add a little salt, then stir in the water until a dough forms.

10 Generously butter a 1 litre pudding basin.

11 Place the dough on a lightly floured work surface and roll it into a circle 5mm thick and large enough to line the basin and give a 3cm overhang.

12 Line the basin with the dough. Then trim off the excess pastry and set aside for later.

13 Chill the lined basin for 20 minutes, then fill it with the beef mixture and cover the meat with a little of the gravy.

14 Roll out the pastry trimmings and cut out a circle large enough to cover the filling.

15 Place it over the top and brush some water around the edges.

16 Bring up the overhanging pastry and fold it over the lid, sealing well.

17 Cover and steam the pudding (see page 157, steps 4–8, over a gentle heat for about 2 hours.

18 Set aside to rest for 10 minutes before turning out.

TIPS AND IDEAS

■ Make sure the meat is well seasoned before putting it in the lined pudding basin.

■ Be careful not to overfill the basin with the meat mixture, and remember to pleat the greaseproof paper and foil. This allows the pudding to expand.

■ When making a savoury suet pudding, you are effectively putting a well-flavoured stew into a pastry case. But make sure it's not too wet and the meat is only just cooked. You can use your favourite stew, including vegetarian ones.

■ The reason I like to cook the meat rather than adding it raw is that using raw meat creates too much thin juice. Also, the flavour is nowhere near as good. By making a stew first, you can thicken the juices and make sure the flavour is just as you like.

■ A steamed pudding is a lovely way to eat thrifty cuts that need long, slow cooking, such as oxtail.

■ Suet pastry is one of the easiest pastries to roll out. If it tears at all, just patch it together.

■ The pastry is better soft rather than too dry – add a little more water if necessary.

■ To line the basin, roll the pastry into a circle, fold it gently in half, then in half again to make a triangle. Put the point of the triangle on the base of the pudding basin and then unfold it, pressing the pastry into the edge of the basin.

■ Don't be tempted to add too much gravy to the pudding. The excess can be reheated and served on the side.

■ The reason for leaving the pudding to sit for 10 minutes before turning it out is that it allows the flavours to settle.

■ For an incomparable flavour, ask your butcher to give you fresh beef suet. You will have to grate it at home, which is a bit of a faff, but well worth it.

RABBIT, KIDNEY AND SULTANA PUDDINGS

I originally made this for the 'The Alan Titchmarsh Show', when I wanted to develop a new savoury pudding. It has proved to be one of my most popular recipes.

Serves 8

4 tablespoons sultanas

Grand Marnier liqueur for soaking

1 large farmed rabbit, boned (use the bones to make stock)

50g plain flour seasoned with sea salt and black pepper

olive oil for frying

1 medium onion, finely sliced

2 rashers of bacon, finely diced

15g unsalted butter, plus extra for greasing

2 lambs' kidneys, quartered

125ml red wine

300ml rabbit stock or chicken stock

2 bay leaves

1 tablespoon thyme leaves

For the pastry:

400g plain flour

½ teaspoon baking powder

1 teaspoon sea salt

175g shredded suet

180ml boiling water

1 Put the sultanas in a bowl, cover with Grand Marnier and set aside to soak.

2 Cut the rabbit meat into 2cm pieces and toss it in the seasoned flour. Heat a little oil in a frying pan and brown the meat on all sides. Transfer it to a casserole dish.

3 Wipe out the frying pan with kitchen paper, add a little oil and fry the onion until soft. Add to the rabbit. Fry the bacon in the same pan and add to the rabbit. Melt the butter in the frying pan and fry the kidneys until brown outside but still pink inside. Set aside.

4 Pour the wine into the frying pan and stir well to deglaze, scraping up any bits stuck to the bottom. Add the liquid to the rabbit mixture, then pour in the stock, add the herbs and mix well. Bring to the boil, cover the casserole dish and put into an oven preheated to 180°C/Gas Mark 4 for about 40 minutes.

5 Add the sultanas, their soaking liquid and the kidneys to the casserole, then return to the oven for another 20–25 minutes, until the meat is tender. Season well with salt and pepper and set aside to cool, then strain the sauce from the meat, reserving it as gravy for later.

6 To make the pastry, put all the dry ingredients into a bowl and mix well. Gradually add the boiling water, mixing until a smooth dough forms.

7 Place the dough on a lightly floured work surface, shape it into a log, then cut into 8 equal pieces. Roll them into circles large enough to line 8 buttered 150g pudding basins, leaving a 5mm overhang. Cut off the excess pastry and set it aside.

8 Spoon the filling into the basins until three-quarters full. Roll out the pastry trimmings and cut out 8 circles to cover the filling. Place them on top and brush some water around the edges. Bring up the overhanging pastry and fold it over each lid to seal well.

9 Cover the puddings (see page 157, steps 4–5) and place them on a rack in a deep baking tin. Pour cold water under the rack, making sure it doesn't actually touch the basins. Cover the whole tray in foil and place in an oven preheated to 180°C/Gas Mark 4 for 1 hour.

10 Turn out the puddings and serve with the hot reserved gravy and mashed parsnips.

BISCUITS

There is hardly an occasion that isn't improved by a homemade biscuit. They are so quick and easy to make and can be as rustic or refined as you like. We have such a great repertoire of biscuit recipes in the UK that it was very difficult deciding which to include here — and, of course, it was also essential to make room for classics from other countries, such as Italian biscotti and French tuiles. Biscuits and cookies tend to be talked about interchangeably these days but, to me, cookies are big, American-style affairs with a chewy centre. The epitome of a classic British biscuit, on the other hand, is the thin ginger biscuit (see page 176).

This is a very basic biscuit recipe that can serve as a template for lots of different flavourings and variations — see page 172 for some ideas to get you started.

BUTTER BISCUITS

To make the butter biscuit dough, follow steps 1 to 2

MAKES 20–24

150g soft unsalted butter

125g caster sugar

250g plain flour

¼ teaspoon bicarbonate of soda

1 egg yolk

2 tablespoons milk

1 teaspoon vanilla extract

golden granulated sugar for rolling

1 Beat the butter until pale, then add the caster sugar and beat again.

2 Add the flour, bicarbonate of soda, egg yolk, milk and vanilla, mixing until a thick paste forms.

3 Shape the paste into a log about 5cm in diameter, wrap in cling film and chill for 3 hours.

4 Unwrap the chilled log and roll in granulated sugar.

5 Cut into 5mm slices and place on a baking parchment-lined baking sheet, spacing them about 2cm apart to allow for expansion.

6 Bake in an oven preheated to 190°C/Gas Mark 5 for 12–15 minutes, until golden. Cool on the baking sheet or a wire rack.

butter biscuit variations

Ginger Butter Biscuits – add 100g very finely chopped crystallised ginger to the basic dough as on page 170, step 2, then roll and bake as in steps 3–6.

Lemon Butter Biscuits – add the zest of 2 lemons to the basic dough as on page 170, step 2, then roll and bake as before.

Cherry Butter Biscuits – add 220g very finely chopped glacé cherries to the basic dough as on page 170, step 2, then roll and bake as before.

Walnut Butter Biscuits – add 150g chopped walnuts to the basic dough as on page 170, step 2, then roll and bake as before.

Pistachio Butter Biscuits – roll the chilled log in 150g chopped pistachios as on page 170, step 4, then slice and bake as before.

Hazelnut Butter Biscuits – add 50g coarsely chopped hazelnuts and 1 tablespoon coarsely ground oats to the basic dough as on page 170, step 2, then roll and bake as before.

TIPS AND IDEAS

■ These biscuits will keep well for up to one week in an airtight container.

■ You can freeze the log of dough, well wrapped, and then either thaw out the whole thing or slice off what you need from the frozen block and return it to the freezer.

■ Chilling the dough thoroughly before cooking makes it easier to slice and helps the biscuits keep their shape in the oven.

■ For neat slices, you can cut directly through the cling film when you slice the dough and then remove it.

■ You could make a triangular or square log, if you prefer, to give different-shaped biscuits.

■ Instead of granulated sugar, try rolling the chilled dough in demerara sugar for a crunchier coating.

■ Do not be tempted to overcook the biscuits. They should be a very pale golden brown when you take them out of the oven. They will continue to firm up as they cool.

■ The dough could be flavoured with cinnamon, caraway seeds, lavender or citrus zest, stirred in with the flour, or with flavouring essences, added to the milk.

■ To make chocolate biscuits, remove 2 tablespoons of the flour and replace with sifted cocoa powder.

■ You could half dip the biscuits in melted chocolate once they are cooked and cooled.

SIMPLE THIN SHORTBREAD

Only three ingredients and the easiest possible recipe to make. It's a good one to start children baking.

Makes 12

225g plain flour, plus extra for dusting

150g unsalted butter, melted and cooled

75g caster sugar

1 Combine all the ingredients until they form a smooth dough.

2 On a lightly floured work surface, roll out the dough to a thickness of 3mm, then stamp out circles using a 6cm cutter. Place them on a baking parchment-lined baking sheet and bake in an oven preheated to 150°C/Gas Mark 2 for about 25 minutes, until pale golden brown. Cool on the baking sheet or a wire rack.

SHORTBREAD FINGERS

You can buy a special docker for pricking shortbread, which makes it much easier. This recipe can be used as the base for Millionaire's Shortbread (see page 174).

Makes 14

200g plain flour, plus extra for dusting

20g rice flour

150g soft unsalted butter, plus extra for greasing

35g caster sugar, plus extra for sprinkling

1 Sift the 2 flours together into a bowl. In a separate bowl, cream the butter and sugar together until pale and fluffy. Add the flours and mix well until a smooth dough forms.

2 On a lightly floured work surface, roll out the dough to fit a buttered shallow 20 x 33cm baking tin, about 5mm deep, and chill for 1 hour.

3 Using a fork, prick the dough all over, then cut into fingers measuring about 2 x 6cm. Bake in an oven preheated to 150°C/Gas Mark 2 for about 35 minutes, until lightly brown. Cool in the tray, and sprinkle with caster sugar before serving.

MILLIONAIRE'S SHORTBREAD

If you love caramel, this is the biscuit for you. Try to resist cutting it before the chocolate has set.

Makes 12

1 quantity Shortbread Fingers, cooled in the tin (see page 173)

300g dark chocolate (60–70% cocoa solids), broken into pieces

For the caramel:

150g unsalted butter

150g caster sugar

397g condensed milk

3 tablespoons golden syrup

1 Put all the caramel ingredients into a wide, shallow, non-stick pan and heat until the mixture starts to turn pale brown – about 10 minutes. Pour it over the shortbread in the tin and leave until cool but not quite set – about 1 hour.

2 Melt the chocolate in a heatproof bowl set over a saucepan of boiling water (the bowl must not actually touch the water). Pour the chocolate over the caramel-topped shortbread and set aside until completely cold. Cut into squares or rectangles to serve.

PARMESAN SHORTBREAD CANAPÉS

Really quick to make – you just whiz everything together in a food processor – these are great served with drinks, or with fish or salad starters.

Makes 18–20

60g plain flour, plus extra for dusting

45g cold unsalted butter, diced

60g Parmesan cheese, freshly grated

sea salt and cayenne pepper

1 Place all the ingredients in a bowl or food processor and mix or whiz until a smooth dough forms. Chill for 5 minutes.

2 On a lightly floured work surface, roll out the dough to a thickness of 5mm. Using a round 3cm cutter, stamp out circles of dough. Place them on baking parchment-lined baking sheets, spacing them 2cm apart, and chill for 30 minutes.

3 Bake the canapés in an oven preheated to 180°C/ Gas Mark 4 for about 8 minutes, until light golden brown. Cool on the baking sheets or a wire rack.

OAT BISCUITS

I made these biscuits regularly when I lived in Scotland. They are plain but extremely good.

Makes 20

150g caster sugar

150g porridge oats

75g wholemeal flour

2 teaspoons wheatgerm

1 teaspoon baking powder

125g soft unsalted butter

1 egg

1 Mix all the dry ingredients together in a bowl. In a separate large bowl, whisk the butter until pale, then add the egg and whisk again. Add the dry mixture and stir until a soft paste forms.

2 Place teaspoonfuls of the paste on a baking parchment-lined baking sheet, spacing them at least 2.5cm apart, and flatten them with the palm of your hand. Bake in an oven preheated to 200°C/Gas Mark 6 for about 15 minutes, until golden brown. Cool on the baking sheet or a wire rack.

---

oaty biscuits variation

Savoury Oaty Biscuits – put 130g diced cold salted butter into a bowl with 350g medium oatmeal, 110g plain flour, 25g oat bran, 1 teaspoon bicarbonate of soda, 1 teaspoon salt and 1 teaspoon caster sugar. Process or rub together until the mixture resembles breadcrumbs. Add 3 tablespoons water and mix well to form a dough. Roll out on a lightly floured surface to a thickness of roughly 4mm, taking care as the dough is brittle. Cut into 20–25 squares, depending on how big you want the biscuits. Transfer to a hot baking sheet and bake in an oven preheated to 180°C/Gas Mark 4 for 20 minutes, until pale golden brown.

OATY BISCUITS

If I had to choose my favourite biscuit recipe, it would probably be this one. I have adapted it slightly from a recipe given to me by a Yorkshire lady.

Makes 25–30

150g soft unsalted butter

150g caster sugar

1 tablespoon golden syrup

150g self-raising flour

120g porridge oats

2 tablespoons milk

1 teaspoon bicarbonate of soda

1 Cream the butter and sugar together. Add the syrup, mix well, then add the flour, oats, milk and bicarbonate of soda. Mix again until a dough forms.

2 Roll the dough into walnut-sized pieces and place them on a parchment-lined baking sheet, spacing them at least 2.5cm apart, and flatten them with the palm of your hand. Bake in an oven preheated to 180°C/Gas Mark 4 for 15–20 minutes. Clap down the biscuits with the bottom of a saucepan to flatten them a bit, then allow to cool on the baking sheet or a wire rack.

GINGER BISCUITS

There are many different ways of making ginger biscuits. This is the crisp, slender, brittle variety — perfect with a cup of tea.

Makes 32

75g unsalted butter

1 tablespoon golden syrup

175g self-raising flour

115g caster sugar

3 teaspoons ground ginger

½ teaspoon bicarbonate of soda

1 egg yolk, beaten

1 Put the butter and golden syrup in a small saucepan and heat gently until melted. Allow to cool until lukewarm.

2 Mix all the dry ingredients together in a bowl. Add the butter mixture and egg yolk and mix well until a dough forms.

3 Take spoonfuls of the dough and roll into walnut-sized balls. Place them on baking parchment-lined baking sheets, spacing them at least 2cm apart and flatten them with the palm of your hand. Bake in an oven preheated to 180°C/Gas Mark 4 for 15–20 minutes, until golden brown. Cool on the baking sheets or a wire rack.

ORANGE AND HAZELNUT BISCUITS

These are delicately scented biscuits with a delightful nuttiness.

Makes 20–24

250g caster sugar

250g plain flour

grated zest and juice of 2 oranges (100ml)

125g unsalted butter, melted and cooled

125g hazelnuts, chopped

1 Combine the sugar and flour in a bowl, then stir in the orange zest and juice. Mix in the melted butter and hazelnuts. Wrap the dough in cling film and chill for at least 4 hours.

2 Break off pieces of the chilled dough and roll into balls the size of a small walnut. Place on a baking parchment-lined baking sheet, spacing them at least 2.5cm apart, and flatten them with the palm of your hand. Bake in an oven preheated to 180°C/Gas Mark 4 for about 12 minutes, until golden brown. Cool on the baking sheets or a wire rack.

CHOCOLATE CHIP COOKIES

These are very chocolatey indeed. Use the recipe as a template for other cookies, substituting different flavourings, nuts and/or dried fruit for the chocolate.

Makes 20–24

200g soft unsalted butter

200g soft light brown sugar

350g plain flour

1 teaspoon baking powder

5g cocoa powder

1 egg

1 teaspoon vanilla extract

zest of 1 orange

50g walnuts, crushed

160g dark chocolate (60–70% cocoa solids), cut into small pieces

1 Whisk the butter in a large mixing bowl until pale and fluffy, then whisk in the sugar. Add half the flour with the baking powder and cocoa powder and mix well. Beat in the egg, then stir in the vanilla. Add the remaining flour along with the orange zest, walnuts and chocolate bits and mix well.

2 Place rounded teaspoonfuls of the mixture on a baking parchment-lined baking sheet, spacing them 2.5cm apart, and flatten them with the palm of your hand. Bake in an oven preheated to 190°C/Gas Mark 5 for 10 minutes, until slightly brown at the edges. Cool on the baking sheet or a wire rack.

CHOCOLATE BROWNIE BISCUITS

These have all the gorgeous flavour and texture of a brownie but translated into biscuit form.

Makes 12

2 eggs

130g caster sugar

½ tablespoon strong black coffee

20g unsalted butter, cut into pieces

200g dark chocolate (60–70% cocoa solids), broken into pieces

40g plain flour

¼ teaspoon baking powder

a pinch of sea salt

50g macadamia nuts, cut in half

50g white chocolate, chopped

1 Whisk together the eggs, sugar and coffee for 7–8 minutes, or until thick and lighter in colour. Set aside.

2 Put the butter and dark chocolate in a heatproof bowl set over a saucepan of simmering water and stir until melted. Set aside to cool for 5 minutes, then add the egg mixture and stir well. Carefully sift in the flour, baking powder and salt, then fold in the nuts and white chocolate.

3 Place spoonfuls of the mixture on 1 or 2 very shallow baking trays lined with greaseproof paper, spacing them at least 2.5cm apart, and flatten them with the palm of your hand. Bake in an oven preheated to 180°C/Gas Mark 4 for 10 minutes, or until risen but still soft in the centre with the top slightly cracked. Transfer to a wire rack to cool and harden.

FIG AND GINGER ROLLS

An old-fashioned favourite with a modern twist. I love ginger and it works well with the sweetness of the figs.

Makes 14

150g dried figs, stemmed and diced

3 pieces of crystallised ginger, diced

50g currants

juice of 1 orange

250ml water

1 egg, beaten

For the pastry:

150g plain flour, plus extra for dusting

75g cold unsalted butter, cut into small pieces

75g caster sugar

a pinch of sea salt

1½ tablespoons water

1 Place the figs, ginger, currants, orange juice and water into a saucepan and bring to the boil. Lower the heat and simmer for about 15 minutes, or until most of the water has evaporated. Set aside to cool.

2 To make the pastry, put the flour and butter into a bowl or food processor and mix or pulse until the mixture resembles fine breadcrumbs. Add the sugar, salt and water and mix or process again to form a dough. Wrap in cling film and chill for 30 minutes.

3 On a lightly floured work surface, roll the dough into a 35 x 12cm rectangle. Place on a chopping board and arrange the fig mixture down the centre of the pastry. Fold one flap of pastry over the top, brush with beaten egg, then fold the other flap of pastry over it. Carefully turn the roll over so that the pastry seam is on the bottom. Chill for 2 hours, until firm.

4 Cut the chilled roll into 6cm slices and place, seam-side down, on a baking parchment-lined baking sheet. Bake in an oven preheated to 180°C/Gas Mark 4 for 20–25 minutes, until golden brown. Cool on the baking sheet or a wire rack.

COCONUT BISCUITS

These biscuits contain no added fat — though it has to be said they're delicious with chocolate drizzled over the top, or just dipped into melted chocolate.

Makes 10

70g desiccated coconut

90g caster sugar

4 tablespoons chopped almonds

2 tablespoons plain flour

1 egg

1 Combine all the ingredients in a bowl and mix with your hands until a dough forms.

2 Break off small pieces of the dough and roll into balls the size of a walnut. Place them on a baking parchment-lined baking sheet, spacing them at least 2.5cm apart, and flatten them with the palm of your hand.

3 Bake in an oven preheated to 180°C/Gas Mark 4 for 15–20 minutes, until pale golden. Cool on the baking sheet or a wire rack.

ORANGE CRISPS

I use these an awful lot to garnish desserts such as ice creams, mousses and fools. They keep very well in an airtight tin.

Makes 24–30

1 large orange

4 tablespoons sugar

3 tablespoons water

1 Cut the orange in half lengthways and slice each half very finely into crescent shapes.

2 Put the sugar and water in a small saucepan and heat together, stirring constantly, until it becomes a syrup.

3 Dip the orange slices into the syrup and place them on a baking parchment-lined baking sheet. Bake in an oven preheated to 120°C/Gas Mark ½ for about 1 hour 20 minutes, until they are crisp and slightly browned. Cool on the baking sheet or a wire rack.

CROQUANTE THINS

These make a lovely accompaniment to ice creams and other desserts. The trick is to cook the mixture to a good golden brown caramel — be careful not to let it burn, though, or it will be bitter.

Makes 36

150g fondant sugar

100g liquid glucose

100g nibbed almonds

1 Put the fondant sugar and glucose in a small saucepan, heat gently until melted, then continue heating until the mixture caramelises.

2 Add the almonds to the caramel, then quickly pour the mixture on to a baking parchment-lined baking sheet. Set aside until cold and hard (do not put in the fridge).

3 Crush the caramel to a fine powder in a food processor or blender. Sprinkle the powder in 5cm circles on a baking parchment-lined baking sheet, spacing them at least 2cm apart. Bake in an oven preheated to 180°C/Gas Mark 4 for about 12 minutes, until golden brown. Cool on the baking sheet or a wire rack. The croquantes will keep for 2 weeks in an airtight tin.

AMARETTI

A quick and easy way to make the classic, paper-wrapped biscuits. This recipe makes soft amaretti rather than the crunchy ones.

Makes 16–18

125g ground hazelnuts

125g ground almonds

225g caster sugar

3 egg whites

1 Combine the nuts and 100g of the sugar in a large bowl. Add the egg whites and mix well. Cover the bowl with cling film and chill for 12 hours, or until the mixture is firm.

2 Put the remaining 125g sugar in a shallow dish. Using 2 teaspoons, form small balls of the nut mixture and drop them into the sugar. Shake the dish to coat the balls evenly, then place them on 2 baking parchment-lined baking sheets, spacing them about 2.5cm apart.

3 Bake in an oven preheated to 180°C/Gas Mark 4 for 12–15 minutes, until golden brown. Cool on the baking sheets or a wire rack.

BRANDY SNAP TUBES OR BASKETS

Everyone loves brandy snaps. These can also be stamped out with a pastry cutter to make little discs.

Makes about 24

100g soft unsalted butter

100g caster sugar

85g plain flour

100g golden syrup

1 Whisk the butter until pale. Add the sugar, whisk again, then add the flour and whisk well.

2 Put the golden syrup into a small saucepan and heat until just runny. Add to the flour mixture and whisk until thick. Cover the bowl with cling film and chill for 4 hours.

3 Put a teaspoonful of the chilled mixture into the palm of your hand, roll into a ball and place on a baking parchment-lined baking sheet. Repeat with the rest of the mixture, spacing the balls at least 6cm apart. Bake in an oven preheated to 180°C/Gas Mark 4 for 10 minutes, or until pale golden brown.

4 While the brandy snaps are still warm, shape them into tubes by rolling them around the handle of a wooden spoon, or make baskets by draping them over inverted ramekins or cups; they will solidify as they cool.

Tuiles is the French word for tiles, and these biscuits are traditionally served curved like roof tiles. These are so thin that you can almost see through them. They make a perfect partner for ice creams and sorbets, and are also very good with a cup of coffee after a meal.

ORANGE AND SESAME SEED TUILES

To curl the tuiles, follow steps 7 to 9

MAKES 20–24

250g caster sugar

100g plain flour

grated zest and juice of 2 oranges (100ml)

125g unsalted butter, melted and cooled

20g ground almonds

125g sesame seeds

1 Mix the sugar and flour in a bowl. Add the orange zest

2 Pour in the orange juice and the melted butter, then add the ground almonds.

3 Mix well, then fold in the sesame seeds. Cover the bowl with cling film and chill for at least 4 hours to firm up.

4 Take walnut-sized pieces of the chilled dough and roll into balls.

5 Place just a few on a baking parchment-lined baking sheet, spacing them well apart.

6 Flatten them briskly with your fingertips. Bake in an oven preheated to 180°C/Gas Mark 4 for about 12 minutes, until golden brown.

7 Allow the tuiles to cool on the baking sheet for 30 seconds.

8 Then lift off with a palette knife and drape them around a rolling pin for just a few seconds to develop a curl.

9 Set them aside on a wire rack to cool, then bake and curl the remaining dough in the same way.

TIPS AND IDEAS

■ You can make the mixture the night before and leave it in the fridge.

■ These work best made on a silicone mat, but if you don't have one, line the baking sheet with baking parchment instead.

■ When you shape the mixture, handle it as little as possible – just shape it lightly with your hand, put it on the baking mat or sheet, then bash with the flat of your hand.

■ The classic mistake is to make these too big. Keep the balls of dough small because they expand a lot in the oven. It's important to bake just 3 or 4 at a time so that they don't spread into each other. This also means you can shape them in small batches, which is easier than trying to cope with a lot at once.

■ Professionals sometimes use special tuile tins for shaping the biscuits, but a rolling pin works very well. If you have a baguette tin, you can shape them round that instead.

■ To make the tuiles into baskets, drape each one over an upturned dariole mould. You can then fill them with ice cream, sorbet or fresh fruit.

■ If the tuiles start to go hard on the baking sheet, you can return them to the oven for a few seconds to soften up.

■ You could use lemon instead of orange.

COCONUT AND ORANGE TUILES

The method below uses a food processor, but please note that the biscuits can also be made by hand.

Makes 20–24

75g desiccated coconut

75g icing sugar, sifted

25g plain flour

zest of 1 orange

2 large egg whites

50g unsalted butter, melted and cooled

1 Blitz half the coconut in a food processor until finely chopped but not reduced to a powder. Add the sugar, flour, orange zest and the remaining coconut and process for just a few seconds to combine. Add the egg whites and melted butter, and process again to mix thoroughly.

2 Transfer the mixture to a bowl, cover with cling film and chill for at least 4 hours to firm up.

3 Place teaspoonfuls of the chilled mixture on a baking parchment-lined baking sheet, spreading them thinly with a palette knife, and spacing them 3cm apart.

4 Bake and curl as on page 185, steps 6–9.

PINEAPPLE TUILES

These are slightly more substantial than the basic tuiles but absolutely delicious.

Makes 14–20

2 egg whites

100g caster sugar

40g plain flour

50g crystallised pineapple, chopped

35g unsalted butter, melted and cooled, plus extra for greasing

sifted icing sugar for dredging

1 Whisk the egg whites and caster sugar until frothy, then fold in the flour, pineapple and melted butter. Cover the bowl with cling film and chill for at least 4 hours to firm up.

2 Place rounded teaspoonfuls of the chilled mixture on a baking parchment-lined baking sheet, spacing them at least 2.5cm apart. Flatten them slightly with your fingertips. Dredge with icing sugar.

3 Bake in an oven preheated to 180°C/Gas Mark 4 for 5–10 minutes, until golden brown. Curl and cool as on page 185, steps 7–9.

POPPY SEED AND GINGER TUILES

I always think these look terribly pretty, thanks to the poppy seeds.

Makes about 30

4 egg whites

200g caster sugar

100g plain flour

20g poppy seeds

1 teaspoon ground ginger

75g unsalted butter, melted and cooled, plus extra for greasing

1 Whisk the egg whites and sugar until frothy, then fold in the flour, poppy seeds, ginger and melted butter. Cover the bowl with cling film and chill for at least 4 hours to firm up.

2 Place rounded teaspoonfuls of the chilled mixture on a baking parchment-lined baking sheet, spacing them at least 4cm apart.

3 Bake in an oven preheated to 200°C/Gas Mark 6 for about 8 minutes, or until golden. Curl and cool as on page 185, steps 7–9.

COFFEE TUILES

These are made in one large sheet and broken into shards. Be sure to spread the mixture out really thinly on the baking sheet.

Makes 15–20

50g plain flour

50g icing sugar, sifted

50g unsalted butter, melted and cooled

1 egg

4 teaspoons finely ground coffee beans

1 Mix the flour and icing sugar in a bowl, then add the melted butter. Whisk in the egg and coffee, then cover the bowl with cling film and chill for at least 4 hours to firm up.

2 Using a slightly damp palette knife, spread the chilled mixture out thinly on a baking parchment-lined baking sheet. Bake in an oven preheated to 180°C/Gas Mark 4 for about 15 minutes, until crisp. Cool on the baking sheet, then break pieces off the finished tuile sheet as required.

CIGARETTE TUILES

There's no denying that these can be tricky to shape, but try to work quickly and you'll soon get the hang of it.

Makes 30

100g soft unsalted butter

100g icing sugar, sifted, plus extra for sprinkling

3 egg whites

75g plain flour

1 Whisk the butter until very pale, then gradually incorporate the icing sugar.

2 Add the egg whites one by one, whisking thoroughly, then add the flour and mix well. Cover the bowl with cling film and chill for at least 4 hours to firm up.

3 Cut a rectangle from the lid of an empty ice cream carton, and cut an 8cm oval or any shape you like out of the middle – the hole will act as a template for the tuiles. Place the template on a baking parchment-lined baking sheet and use a palette knife to spread a very thin layer of the chilled mixture over the hole. Lift up the template and repeat this step to make 3 more tuiles. (I recommend you do only about 4 at a time because they are quite hard to work with.) Bake in an oven preheated to 180°C/Gas Mark 4 for 7–10 minutes, until pale golden brown.

4 Lift the tuiles off the sheet one at a time and place close to the edge of a work surface. Position the handle of a wooden spoon on the tuile at right angles to the surface edge and quickly roll the tuile around the handle from left to right to make a cigarette shape. Repeat with the remaining tuiles, and sprinkle with sifted icing sugar before serving.

These are at least twice as good as the biscotti you can buy, but half the price. Biscotti means 'twice cooked'. The biscuit dough is shaped into a log, baked, then sliced and baked again. They are lovely to give as presents, packaged in an attractive bag or box.

⤙ BISCOTTI DI PRATO ⤚

To shape the biscotti, follow steps 5 to 11

MAKES ABOUT 40 BISCUITS

250g plain flour, plus extra for dusting

150g caster sugar

a pinch of sea salt

½ teaspoon baking powder

1 egg, plus 1 egg yolk

50g unsalted butter, melted and cooled, plus extra for greasing

1 teaspoon grated orange zest

50g whole blanched almonds

1 egg yolk, for brushing

1 Pour the flour on to a work surface to form a mound.

2 Make a well in the centre and add the sugar, salt, baking powder, whole egg and egg yolk, melted butter and orange zest.

3 Gradually work the flour into the wet ingredients with a fork until a dryish dough forms.

4 Now work it by hand – no kneading – and add the almonds.

5 Cut the dough in half, place on a work surface.

6 Roll each piece into a log about 30cm long and 3cm in diameter.

7 Place the logs on a large baking parchment-lined baking sheet (at least 37cm long), spacing them at least 5cm apart.

8 Beat the egg yolk and brush over the dough logs.

9 Bake in an oven preheated to 180°C/ Gas Mark 4 for 15 minutes, then lower the heat to 160°C/Gas Mark 3 and bake for a further 20 minutes.

10 Cut each of the logs diagonally into 1cm slices

11 Spread them out on the baking sheet and return them to the oven for another 3 minutes.

12 Turn them over, bake for 3 more minutes, then transfer to a wire rack until cold.

BISCUITS

TIPS AND IDEAS

■ Don't be tempted to make the biscotti dough in an electric mixer. I find the biscuits are so much better if you make it by hand.

■ When you work the mixture you need to bring it together into a smooth paste, but don't overdo it. The less you handle it the better.

■ When cutting the logs, be sure to use a serrated knife and a sawing motion to give a very clean cut, otherwise the slices will fall apart.

■ The slices should be baked until they are very pale brown and have a slightly cakey texture. They will firm up more as they cool.

■ The biscotti will keep in an airtight tin for at least 3 weeks.

■ The traditional way to serve biscotti is with a glass of vin santo for dipping. A luxurious alternative is to give everyone a little bowl of melted chocolate instead.

biscotti variations

Pistachio Biscotti – make the basic biscotti dough as on pages 190–191, steps 1–4, but omit the almonds and work 50g unsalted skinned pistachios into the dough in step 4. Shape, bake and slice as before.

Cherry and Walnut Biscotti – make the basic biscotti dough as on pages 190–191, steps 1–4, but using 1 teaspoon baking powder rather than the previous amount and 50ml vegetable oil rather than the butter. Add 1½ teaspoons vanilla extract in step 2. Omit the almonds and work 50g finely chopped walnuts, 130g chopped dried sour cherries and 2 teaspoons grated orange zest into the dough in step 4. Shape as before, then brush with 1 egg white beaten with 1 teaspoon water and sprinkle with 1 tablespoon granulated sugar. Bake and slice as before.

Dark Chocolate Biscotti – make the basic biscotti dough as on pages 190–191, steps 1–4, but using ¼ teaspoon salt and 1 teaspoon baking powder instead of the previous amounts, adding 1½ teaspoons vanilla extract and omitting the orange zest in step 2. Omit the almonds and work in 150g dark chocolate chips in step 4. Shape as before, then brush with 1 egg white beaten with 1 teaspoon water rather than the egg yolk. Bake and slice as before.

SOUTHERN CHEESE BISCUITS

I love savoury biscuits and these are very easy to make.

Makes 30

200g plain flour, plus extra for dusting

225g Cheddar cheese, grated

110g unsalted butter, cut into small pieces

sea salt and cayenne pepper

1 Put all the ingredients into a bowl or food processor and mix or blitz until a dough forms. Place it on a lightly floured surface and shape into a log about 3cm in diameter. Wrap in cling film and chill for 1 hour.

2 Slice the chilled log into circles about 3mm thick and place on a baking parchment-lined baking sheet, spacing them about 2cm apart. Bake in an oven preheated to 180°C/Gas Mark 4 for about 15 minutes, until brown and crispy.

ROSEMARY DIGESTIVE BISCUITS

This is a classic digestive biscuit but I've added fresh rosemary — one of my favourite ingredients, not surprisingly!

Makes 12

175g wholemeal flour

25g ground oats

a large pinch of sea salt

25g plain flour, plus extra for dusting

35g caster sugar

1 teaspoon baking powder

1 tablespoon finely chopped rosemary

75g unsalted butter, cut into small pieces

milk for binding

1 Put all the dry ingredients into a bowl, rub in the butter, then add just enough milk to bind the mixture together and form a dough.

2 On a lightly floured work surface, roll the dough out thinly, then stamp out circles using a 6cm cutter. Prick them all over with a fork.

3 Place on baking parchment-lined baking sheets, spacing them 2cm apart, and bake in an oven preheated to 180°C/Gas Mark 4 for about 25 minutes. Do not over-bake. Cool on the baking sheet or a wire rack.

cheese biscuit variation

Cheese and Nut Biscuits – add 100g chopped walnuts and/or sesame or poppy seeds to the basic dough.

ITALIAN MERINGUE

Italian meringue is what is known as a 'cooked' meringue. The egg whites are effectively cooked by pouring a hot sugar syrup on to them while whisking, causing them to expand and become thick and glossy. This means you don't need to cook the meringue any further and it is much more stable than ordinary meringue. Where ordinary meringue can deflate when mixed with other ingredients, Italian meringue will not lose its volume. It is extremely versatile: mix with flavourings and freeze to make a cheat's ice cream; use it as a base for various mousses; or serve it as a topping.

Here Italian meringue is used to make a lovely soft fruit mousse. It gives a much better texture than simply using whipped egg whites. You could use any soft fruit for this, but it needs to be puréed until really smooth.

PEACH MOUSSE WITH ITALIAN MERINGUE

To make the basic Italian Meringue, follow steps 5 to 13
To make the basic Mousse, follow steps 14 to 20

MAKES 450G MERINGUE AND SERVES 6–8

6g gelatine leaves

250g canned unsweetened peach purée, or whiz drained canned peaches in a blender, then push through a sieve if not smooth enough, plus extra for decoration

50g unsalted butter, cut into small pieces

125g double cream

FOR THE BASE:

90g ground almonds

90g caster sugar

25g icing sugar, sifted

2 eggs

20g unsalted butter, cut into small pieces

25g plain flour

2 egg whites

FOR THE ITALIAN MERINGUE:

4 egg whites

175g caster sugar

3 tablespoons water

1 First make the base. Place the ground almonds, sugars, whole eggs, butter and flour in a bowl and mix well.

2 Whisk the egg whites to soft peaks, then fold into the flour mixture for 30 seconds.

3 Spread the mixture on a baking parchment-lined baking sheet in a layer about 3mm thick.

4 Bake in an oven preheated to 180°C/Gas Mark 4 for 10–15 minutes, until pale golden. Set aside on the baking sheet until cold.

5 To make the meringue, put the egg whites in a freestanding electric mixer and set aside.

6 Meanwhile, put the sugar and water into a small pan.

7 Insert a sugar thermometer and place over a low heat until the sugar has melted.

8 When the sugar starts to crystalllise, use a pastry brush dipped in water to brush the sides of the pan and stop the mixture from crystallising.

9 When the sugar has melted, boil for 5 minutes, until the temperature reaches 110°C.

10 Meanwhile, turn on the mixer and whisk the egg whites to soft peaks.

11 By the time they are ready, the sugar temperature should have reached 120°C. Remove the saucepan from the heat.

12 Carefully pour the sugar syrup in a steady stream into the egg whites, whisking constantly for about 10 minutes, until the mixture starts to cool.

13 Set aside until needed.

14 To make the mousse, soak the gelatine in a little cold water for 15 minutes.

15 Place one-third of the peach purée in a saucepan over a medium heat.

16 Squeeze the gelatine dry, then add it to the purée, stirring until it has melted.

17 Add the butter and whisk until it is fully incorporated.

18 Put the remaining purée into a large mixing bowl, pour in the peach-gelatine mixture and stir thoroughly.

19 Add 125g of the Italian Meringue to the purée and whisk well.

20 Whisk the cream to very soft peaks, taking care not to overwhip, then fold into the peach mixture.

21 Cut the cooled biscuit base to fit inside the base of a loose-bottomed 21cm cake tin or a ring (about 5cm deep) placed on a baking sheet.

22 Pour in the peach mixture to 1cm below the rim of the tin or ring and chill for about 4 hours.

23 When the mousse has set, use a blowtorch around the edge of the ring for about 30 seconds to help loosen the mousse from the ring.

24 Carefully remove the ring from the mousse. Serve slices of the dessert drizzled with peach purée, if liked.

peach mousse with Italian meringue variations

Dark Chocolate Mousse with Italian Meringue – make the biscuit base and Italian meringues as on pages 198–200, steps 1–13. Put 100ml double cream in a saucepan and bring to the boil. Add 250g dark chocolate (60–70% cocoa solids), broken into pieces, and stir off the heat until melted. Add Grand Marnier or Cointreau liqueur to taste. Whisk 200ml double cream to soft peaks, then fold it into the chocolate mixture and stir gently. Spread over the biscuit base and top with the Italian meringue. This mousse can also be served in ramekins, or shaped into quenelles using 2 spoons.

Mini Mousses with Italian Meringue – wrap greaseproof paper around the outside of 8 small ramekins, making it stand about 5cm above the rim, and use sticky tape or string to hold it in place. Make the biscuit base, Italian meringues and peach mousse as on pages 198–200, steps 1–20. Cut the biscuit base into circles that fit in the bottom of each prepared ramekin, and place the dishes on a baking sheet. Pour in enough mousse to come 1cm below the paper collar and chill for 4 hours, until set. To serve, remove the paper collar and spread the remaining Italian Meringue over each mousse with the back of a spoon. Blowtorch or grill the top to add some colour.

TIPS AND IDEAS

■ There will be some leftover meringue with this recipe, but it's not practical to make a smaller quantity. It will keep, covered, in the fridge overnight. Simply re-whip the next day. Or you can mix it with any flavouring and freeze to make an ice cream.

■ Another way of using up Italian meringue is to place small spoonfuls on a baking parchment-lined baking sheet and bake in an oven preheated to 140°C/Gas Mark 1 for about 20 minutes. Serve these tiny meringues as petits fours or to accompany other desserts, such as ice cream.

■ Make sure the bowl in which you whip the egg whites is completely clean and grease free.

■ It's much easier making Italian meringue in a freestanding electric mixer, though you can use a handheld beater if necessary.

■ When making the sugar syrup, be sure that all the sugar has melted before bringing it to the boil, otherwise it will crystallise. Brushing down the sides of the pan with a clean pastry brush cleans off any stray granules of sugar.

■ Be very careful not to let the sugar syrup become hotter than 120°C, otherwise it will harden.

■ I have a proper copper sugar pan, bought 35 years ago, which I love using for sugar syrup. It comes with me on every demonstration and conducts the heat well. If you don't have a copper pan, be sure to use a pan with a really thick base.

■ Add the sugar syrup to the egg whites in a thin trickle, like adding oil to mayonnaise.

■ The meringue is ready when it is smooth, glossy and very stiff.

■ Be careful not to over-whip the egg whites – they should be standing in soft peaks.

■ To get the correct texture, it's really important to keep beating after adding the syrup.

■ The whole dessert can be frozen and then thawed in the fridge overnight before serving.

WHITE CHOCOLATE MOUSSE AND RHUBARB

A simple white chocolate mousse with rhubarb served on the side. Here it is made into individual mousses, but you could just set it in one large bowl.

Serves 10

4g gelatine leaves

250ml double cream

250g white chocolate, broken into pieces

125g unsalted butter, cut into small pieces

kirsch liqueur, to taste

150g Italian Meringue (see pages 198–200, steps 5–13)

400g rhubarb

50g caster sugar

1 Soak the gelatine in a little cold water for 15 minutes.

2 Meanwhile, pour 150ml of the cream into a saucepan and bring to the boil. Add the chocolate and butter, stirring until both have melted. Squeeze the gelatine dry, then add it to the chocolate mixture with the kirsch, stirring until it has melted. When cool, fold in the Italian Meringue, followed by the remaining cream.

3 Set out 8 small ramekins, or cover one end of 8 individual rings with a double layer of cling film and place them on a board. Pour in the cream mixture and place in the fridge to set.

4 Meanwhile, cut the rhubarb into 4cm chunks, place in a shallow baking tin and sprinkle with the sugar. Bake in an oven preheated to 190°C/Gas Mark 5 for 15–20 minutes, until soft to the point of a knife. Set aside to cool.

5 To serve, remove the rings and cling film, or dip the bases of the ramekins into warm water to loosen the mousse, then turn each one on to a serving plate and surround with the rhubarb.

BLACKCURRANT ICED SOUFFLÉ

A delicious and very pretty little number. Wrapping greaseproof paper round the ramekins and overfilling them is an easy technique to make it appear that the soufflés have risen above the rim of the dish — you simply peel off the paper once the mousse has set.

Serves 6–8

12g gelatine leaves

400g canned blackcurrant purée (If the canned fruit purée seems too runny, mix 1 rounded teaspoon cornflour with a little of the blackcurrant liquid and stir it into the purée. Heat gently to thicken, then use as directed.)

40g unsalted butter, cut into small pieces

300g Italian Meringue (see pages 198–200, steps 5–13)

250ml double cream

1 Soak the gelatine in a little water for 15 minutes. Meanwhile, take 6 small ramekins and tie or tape some greaseproof paper around the outside of each one, ensuring it stands 5cm above the rim.

2 Take one-third of the purée, heat gently to a simmer, then take off the heat. Squeeze the gelatine dry and add it to the purée, stirring until it has dissolved. Stir in the butter until melted, then add the remaining purée. Set aside.

3 Whisk the meringue into the purée. Lightly whip the cream until just holding its shape, then fold it into the purée. Fill the prepared ramekins so that the mixture comes 1cm below the top of the greaseproof collar. Chill for 4 hours and carefully peel off the paper before serving.

blackcurrant iced soufflé variation

Fresh Blackcurrant Purée – top and tail 600g fresh blackcurrants, then rinse and drain well. Whiz in a blender, then push through a fine sieve, discarding all the solids. If the mixture seems a bit thick, add a little water. This method works with all soft fruit, and the quantity used here makes 400g purée. Any excess can be frozen.

NOUGAT PARFAIT

This is a slight variation on Italian meringue, with the sugar syrup made with honey rather than water. I like to serve it with strawberries.

Serves 8

250g flaked almonds

400g caster sugar

3 tablespoons water

75g runny honey

6 egg whites

300ml double cream

1 Brown the flaked almonds by grilling them or heating them in a dry non-stick pan.

2 Put 300g of the caster sugar into a saucepan with the water and heat gently, without stirring, until the sugar has dissolved. Increase the heat until the liquid is a light caramel colour: take care not to overheat it or allow it to become dark. Remove from the heat and mix in the browned almonds, stirring with a wooden spoon. Turn the mixture on to a sheet of oiled baking parchment or a baking mat and allow to cool for 1 hour. Once cold, crush it into tiny pieces using the end of a rolling pin.

3 Line 1 large terrine dish or 8–10 small ramekins with cling film. Put the remaining sugar into a small pan with the honey and heat gently until the sugar has dissolved. Increase the heat and insert a sugar thermometer. When the temperature reaches 110°C, start whisking the egg whites. When soft peaks are formed, slowly pour in the sugar mixture, whisking all the time, until the meringue has cooled.

4 Transfer the meringue to a bowl and stir in the ground caramel. Whip the cream to soft peaks and fold into the meringue. Pour the mixture into the prepared dish(es) and freeze for at least 6 hours.

LEMON AND LIME MERINGUE PIE

One of my favourite desserts of all time. The ideal proportions for this pie are two-thirds lemon and lime filling and one-third meringue, so don't overdo the meringue topping.

Serves 8

5 eggs, plus 1 large egg yolk

200g caster sugar

grated zest of 2 lemons and 65ml juice, strained

grated zest of 1 limes and 65ml juice, strained

175ml double cream

1 blind-baked Sweet Shortcrust Pastry case (see pages 94–96, steps 1–14)

1 quantity Italian Meringue (see pages 198–200, steps 5–13) whisked with 1 tablespoon lime juice

1 Whisk the whole eggs, egg yolk and sugar in a large bowl, add the citrus zest and juice, then whisk in the cream. The mixture will be quite thin. Pour it into the cold pastry case and bake in an oven preheated to 140°C/Gas Mark 1 for about 45 minutes, until just set – it should have a slight movement in the centre. Set aside until completely cold.

2 Spoon the meringue over the lime pie filling, making sure there are no gaps, and freeze any excess meringue. This must be done carefully because the filling is very soft. Blowtorch the top, or place under a hot grill, to add some colour.

PANNA COTTA

The name of this Italian dessert means 'cooked cream' and it really couldn't be simpler. It's just a matter of heating the cream with sugar and then setting it with a little gelatine. Because it's so basic it lends itself to all kinds of flavours, even savoury ones. Although panna cotta is traditionally made in individual dariole moulds, it can also be set in one large dish, then scooped out to serve.

A panna cotta with a tropical flavour. Surprisingly, coconut also goes well with strawberry, so you could try that as an alternative to pineapple — keeping the mango coulis or not, as you wish.

COCONUT PANNA COTTA
with Mango Coulis

To make the basic Panna Cotta, follow steps 1 to 4
To remove the Panna Cotta from a ramekin, follow steps 8 to 9

SERVES 6

9g gelatine leaves

600ml double cream

100g caster sugar

220ml coconut milk

2 tablespoons white rum

8 slices of pineapple, cored

FOR THE MANGO COULIS:

4 tablespoons caster sugar

8 tablespoons water

1 mango, peeled, stoned and whizzed to a purée

juice of 2 oranges

1 Soak the gelatine in a little cold water for 15 minutes, then squeeze it dry.

2 Meanwhile, heat the cream and sugar until almost simmering.

3 Then take off the heat, add the squeezed gelatine and stir until it has completely dissolved.

4 Stir the coconut milk and rum into the cream mixture, then transfer to a jug and pour into 6 small dariole moulds. Set in the fridge for at least 2 hours.

5 To make the coulis, put the sugar and water into a small saucepan and heat until the sugar has dissolved. Boil for 5 minutes to create a syrup.

6 Mix the mango pulp and orange juice into the sugar syrup.

7 To serve, put a ring of pineapple on each serving plate.

8 Dip the bases of the moulds into warm water to loosen the panna cotta.

9 Then invert each one on to a pineapple ring. Surround with the mango coulis.

TIPS AND IDEAS

■ Once you've established the amount of gelatine you need to set panna cotta, you can make up your own flavoured versions. A good rule of thumb is 5g gelatine for 500ml liquid.

■ Be very careful not to let the cream boil after the gelatine has been added, otherwise the gelatine will become stringy. On the other hand, it's important that the cream is hot enough to dissolve the gelatine completely.

■ You can use powdered gelatine if you wish, but I find leaf gelatine a more delicately flavoured product, and easier to use.

■ Gelatine is a meat by-product, but if you are a vegetarian, you can still enjoy panna cotta. Just replace the gelatine with agar agar, following the instructions on the packet.

■ If you are including flavourings such as vanilla seeds, which need to be suspended throughout the panna cotta, add them when the panna cotta is just beginning to thicken, otherwise they will sink to the bottom. Then pour the mixture into the dariole moulds and leave it to set completely.

■ A panna cotta should have a very light set, not a firm one. It should be a light, soft cream, with a wobble to it.

■ You can use other liquids, such as buttermilk or crème fraîche. It's best to use them in combination with cream rather than replacing the cream completely so that the flavour doesn't become overpowering.

■ Panna cotta will keep in the fridge for a couple of days.

■ You could layer panna cotta in different colours – plain, saffron and coffee or chocolate look good together. Simply pour a little of each one into each mould and let it set before adding another layer.

ORANGE FLOWER AND ROSE WATER PANNA COTTA

Rose water varies enormously in strength; some makes are virtually flavourless, so taste before adding it to a recipe.

Serves 6

7g gelatine leaves

500ml double cream

80ml full-fat milk

75g caster sugar

1 tablespoon honey

1 teaspoon rose water

1 teaspoon orange flower water

For the pomegranate syrup:

200g granulated sugar

120ml water

1 tablespoon lemon juice

seeds from 1 pomegranate

2 teaspoons orange flower water

1 Soak the gelatine in a little cold water for 15 minutes, then squeeze it dry. Meanwhile, put 300ml of the cream in a saucepan with the milk, sugar and honey, stir once and bring to a simmer. Take off the heat, add the gelatine and stir until it has completely dissolved. Stir in the rose water and the orange flower water.

2 Whip the remaining cream and fold it into the gelatine mixture. Pour into 6 dariole moulds and set in the fridge for at least 6 hours.

3 To make the syrup, put the sugar and water into a small saucepan, heat until the sugar has dissolved, then boil for 3 minutes. Set aside until cold, then add the lemon juice, pomegranate seeds and orange flower water.

4 To serve, dip the bases of the moulds into warm water to loosen the panna cotta, then invert on to serving plates and drizzle the pomegranate syrup around them.

STILTON PANNA COTTA WITH WALNUTS

This makes a delicious starter. You can use any decent creamy cheese. Goat's cheese and Camembert are particularly good, but blue cheese is my favourite.

Serves 4

3g gelatine leaves

juice of ½ lemon

125g Stilton cheese, crumbled

125g cream cheese

150ml whipping cream, whipped

a large handful of mixed young salad leaves

fine sea salt and white pepper

20 walnut halves, toasted, for garnish

For the dressing:

4 tablespoons walnut oil

2 tablespoons extra virgin olive oil

2 tablespoons red wine vinegar

1 Soak the gelatine in a little cold water for 15 minutes, then squeeze it dry. Meanwhile, put the lemon juice in a saucepan and bring to a simmer. Take the pan off the heat, add the gelatine and stir until it has completely dissolved.

2 Put both cheeses into a bowl and mash with a fork until smooth. Fold in the whipped cream. Season with pepper and a little salt, then fold in the lemon gelatine. Pour the mixture into 4 small dariole moulds and set in the fridge for about 3 hours.

3 To make the dressing, whisk the oils and vinegar together until emulsified.

4 Just before serving, toss the salad leaves in the dressing and arrange them on individual plates. Dip the bases of the moulds into warm water to loosen the panna cotta, then invert on to the leaves. Garnish with the toasted walnuts.

HERB AND CHILLI PANNA COTTA

A lovely summer starter. Basil works well, but do experiment with other herbs, if you like.

Serves 6–8

5g gelatine leaves

juice of ½ lemon

200g cream cheese

50g basil leaves

200ml whipping cream, whipped

10g chives, very finely chopped

1 teaspoon chilli powder

fine sea salt and white pepper

1 Soak the gelatine in a little cold water for 15 minutes, then squeeze it dry. Meanwhile, put the lemon juice in a saucepan and bring to a simmer. Take the pan off the heat, add the gelatine and stir until it has completely dissolved.

2 Whiz the cream cheese and basil in a blender until smooth, then fold in the whipped cream. Season with pepper and a little salt, then fold in the lemon gelatine, chives and chilli powder. Pour the mixture into a bowl and set in the fridge for about an hour.

3 To serve, use 2 spoons to shape quenelles of panna cotta and place on serving plates with toasted bread and mixed leaves.

ICE CREAMS

If you buy an ice cream machine and use
it regularly, you will save an awful lot of money
on ice cream. Moreover, your ice cream will be
free of preservatives and other additives, sweetened
and flavoured the way you like it, and will keep
in the freezer ready for whenever you need it.
Once you have a good basic ice cream recipe it's
very easy to adapt it to different flavours. Most
of the ice creams in this chapter have a custard
base, but the very simplest way to make ice cream
is to mix fruit purée with cream and freeze.

13 Take off the heat and add the remaining water, stirring all the time until thoroughly combined. Take care, as the sugar will spit.

14 Add two-thirds of the caramel to the basic custard.

15 Then cover with cling film as before and set aside until cold.

16 Transfer to an ice cream machine and churn according to the manufacturer's instructions. If making by hand, see the tip below.

17 Heat the remaining caramel with the double cream.

18 Pour the sauce into a jug. Serve with scoops of the finished ice cream, drizzled with the sauce and scattered with chocolate shavings.

TIPS AND IDEAS

■ If you don't have an ice cream machine, pour the mixture into a shallow lidded container and freeze for about an hour, until it is firm around the edges. Remove from the freezer and whisk well to get rid of ice crystals, then return to the freezer. Repeat a couple of times, then freeze until solid.

■ This ice cream starts with making a custard. You can cheat and buy a carton of custard, if you like.

■ If you are worried about the custard curdling, add 2 teaspoons cornflour to the egg yolks and sugar.

■ It's important to strain the custard through a really fine sieve to give a very smooth ice cream.

■ You can replace half the milk in the ice cream with double cream for a richer result.

■ Sometimes I use liquid glucose instead of sugar, which gives the ice cream a smoother texture.

■ If you are adding alcohol to ice cream, be careful not to add too much, otherwise it won't set properly.

■ If making a ripple ice cream, churn the ice cream as usual, then stir in the ripple mixture – a fruit purée, for example – at the end, before freezing.

■ When making caramel, be sure to use a deep pan with a heavy base to prevent burning.

■ Take the caramel to as dark a colour as you dare, but be careful not to let it burn or it will taste bitter. Mahogany is fine – black is not!

■ Resist the temptation to dip your finger in the bubbling caramel; it will give you serious burns. On the subject of safety, never leave a pan of boiling caramel unattended.

■ Before serving ice cream, transfer it to the fridge for 20–30 minutes to soften slightly.

■ If you are putting a scoop of ice cream on a plate, place it on a dusting of icing sugar and it will stay where it is rather than sliding around.

GINGER ICE CREAM

We have a family weakness for ginger and put it into everything. This is one ice cream that is best eaten on its own.

Serves 6

300ml full-fat milk

200ml double cream

2cm piece of fresh ginger, finely grated

8 large egg yolks

150g caster sugar

2 tablespoons kirsch liqueur (optional)

1 tablespoon stem ginger in syrup, very finely chopped

1 Put the milk, cream and grated ginger into a heavy-based saucepan and bring to the boil, stirring constantly. Take off the heat, leave to infuse for 1 hour, then pour through a fine strainer, discarding the solids.

2 Put the egg yolks and sugar into a bowl and whisk with a balloon whisk until smooth and slightly paler. Gradually pour the strained milk and cream into the egg mixture, whisking constantly. Return to the pan, place over a low heat and cook gently, stirring from side to side with a wooden spoon, until the mixture thickens. It is ready when you can draw your finger across the back of the coated spoon and the channel stays clear and does not drip. Take off the heat and add the kirsch (if using) and the stem ginger. Cover with cling film, placing it directly on top of the custard to prevent a skin forming, and set aside to cool.

3 When cold, transfer the mixture to an ice cream machine and churn according to the manufacturer's instructions. If making by hand, see the tip on page 222.

LEMON ICE CREAM

A beautifully refreshing ice cream that goes really well with treacle tart or any frangipane tart.

Serves 6

500ml full-fat milk

200ml double cream

zest and juice of 3 lemons

8 egg yolks

150g caster sugar

1 Put the milk, cream and lemon zest into a heavy-based saucepan and bring to the boil, stirring constantly. Take off the heat, leave to infuse for 1 hour, then pour through a fine strainer, discarding the solids.

2 Put the egg yolks and sugar into a bowl and whisk until smooth and slightly paler. Gradually pour the strained milk and cream into the egg mixture, whisking constantly. Return to the pan, place over a low heat and cook gently, stirring from side to side with a wooden spoon, until the mixture thickens. It is ready when you can draw your finger across the back of the coated spoon and the channel stays clear and does not drip. Take off the heat and stir in the lemon juice. Cover with cling film, placing it directly on top of the custard to prevent a skin forming, and set aside to cool.

3 When cold, transfer the mixture to an ice cream machine and churn according to the manufacturer's instructions. If making by hand, see the tip on page 222.

ORANGE ICE CREAM

This makes a good winter ice cream and is delicious with chocolate desserts. You can also make it with blood oranges for a gorgeous colour.

Serves 6

8 egg yolks

100g caster sugar

500ml full-fat milk

600g oranges

50ml liquid glucose

200g granulated sugar

1 Put the egg yolks and caster sugar into a bowl and whisk with a balloon whisk until smooth and slightly paler.

2 Pour the milk into a saucepan and bring to the boil. Gradually pour it into the egg mixture, whisking all the time. Return the mixture to the pan, place over a low heat and cook gently, stirring from side to side with a wooden spoon, until the mixture thickens. It is ready when you can draw your finger across the back of the coated spoon and the channel stays clear and does not drip. Pour the custard through a fine sieve into a bowl. Cover with cling film, placing it directly on top of the custard to prevent a skin forming, and set aside to cool.

3 Remove the zest from the oranges and cut each fruit in half. Place both zest and fruit in a bowl with the glucose and granulated sugar and leave overnight, or for at least 4 hours. Squeeze the juice from the orange halves into the glucose mixture, stir briefly, then strain through a fine sieve. Add the strained liquid to the cold custard and stir again.

4 Transfer the mixture to an ice cream machine and churn according to the manufacturer's instructions. If making by hand, see the tip on page 222.

PEACH ICE CREAM

You can use nectarines or plums in this recipe too, or even just purée a can of peaches. It's a very simple method, as you don't need to make a custard.

Serves 4

200ml water

150g caster sugar

500g ripe yellow peaches, halved and stoned

2 tablespoons peach schnapps liqueur

100ml double cream

1 Put the water and sugar in a saucepan and bring to the boil. Boil for 2 minutes, then set aside to cool.

2 Skin the peaches (see page 260, step 1), then whiz the flesh in a blender to a purée. Add the cooled syrup and the schnapps and whiz again.

3 Transfer the mixture to an ice cream machine and churn according to the manufacturer's instructions, adding the cream when the mixture is beginning to solidify. If making by hand, see the tip on page 222, again adding the cream when the mixture first begins to solidify.

SORBETS

Sorbets make a wonderful accompaniment
to any dessert and are delicious eaten on their
own too. They are relatively healthy, since they
don't contain any fat, just a little sugar, and
are really easy to make. A lot of sorbet recipes
include just three ingredients — fruit, lemon juice
and sugar — so they stay true to the flavour of
the fruit. Getting the balance of flavours right is
the key thing. Usually the sweetness is balanced
with lemon juice. An overly sweet sorbet can
be cloying, so it's better to err on the side of
tartness. If you want to make a lot of sorbets,
it is worth investing in an ice cream machine to
ensure a smooth texture.

This sorbet is delicious on its own or served with lemon tart.
Make it when raspberries are in season for the best flavour.

RASPBERRY SORBET

To make the basic Sugar Syrup, follow step 1

**MAKES 150ML SUGAR SYRUP
AND THE SORBET SERVES 6**

600g fresh raspberries

juice of 2 lemons

100ml liquid glucose

FOR THE SUGAR SYRUP:

150g caster sugar

150ml water

1 First make the syrup. Put the sugar and water in a saucepan, bring to the boil and boil for 5 minutes.

2 Using the back of a spoon, press the raspberries through a fine sieve into a bowl.

3 Stir in the lemon juice and glucose.

4 Then add the sugar syrup according to taste: if you think the mixture is sweet enough before you have added it all, just stop. Set aside to cool.

5 When cold, transfer the mixture to an ice cream machine.

6 Churn until a soft sorbet has formed (about 30–45 minutes). If making by hand, see the tip on page 222).

FRUIT PUDDINGS

Fruit puddings should celebrate fruit in season
— or in winter, when there is no local fruit, the
best of the tropical fruits, such as pineapples,
mangoes and passion fruit. It's lovely to follow
the seasons, moving from the first forced rhubarb
through to summer berries, peaches and plums,
then apples, pears and quinces. And, of course,
we have citrus fruit available all year round for
desserts such as Lemon Posset (see page 250)
and Orange and Mint Jelly (page 245).

TIPS AND IDEAS

■ No matter what kind of fruit you use in a sorbet, it's always a good idea to push it through a fine sieve after puréeing to make sure it is perfectly smooth.

■ When making the syrup, do ensure that the sugar has completely dissolved before bringing it to the boil, otherwise the sugar will crystallise.

■ If you plan to make a lot of sorbets, you can prepare a large batch of sugar syrup and keep it in the fridge for at least a couple of weeks.

■ Sugar not only sweetens the sorbet but helps to give it a smooth texture. You can reduce the sugar if you like, but the texture won't be as fine.

■ Make sure the sorbet mixture is completely cold before you churn it in an ice cream machine; this minimises the risk of ice crystals forming.

■ To enjoy the fresh flavour of sorbet at its best, try not to keep it in the freezer for more than a week. If you do end up keeping it for longer than this, though, you can freshen it up by letting it melt and then re-churning it.

■ To make a granita instead of a sorbet, freeze the mixture in a plastic freezer box until it is beginning to harden around the edges, then take it out and stir with a fork. Return to the freezer and repeat 3 or 4 times, until you have a tub full of flavoured ice crystals.

■ You can serve a small amount of sorbet between courses at a formal dinner as a palate freshener.

■ Before serving sorbets, transfer them to the fridge for 20–30 minutes to soften slightly.

RASPBERRY AND LAVENDER SORBET

An unusual combination but it really works. If you don't want to make lavender syrup, online stockists are easy to find.

Serves 4

700g fresh raspberries

½ quantity Sugar Syrup (see page 232, step 1)

½ quantity Lavender and Vanilla Syrup (see page 267)

1 Whiz the raspberries in a blender, then push the mixture through a sieve to remove the seeds. You need 500ml raspberry purée.

2 When the sugar syrup is completely cold, add the lavender syrup, then stir in the raspberry purée. Taste and adjust with a little more sugar syrup or lavender syrup if required.

3 Transfer the mixture to an ice cream machine and churn until a soft sorbet has formed (about 30–45 minutes). If making by hand, see the tip on page 222.

STRAWBERRY SORBET

One of the great classics. I love it served with Blood Orange Sorbet (page 236) and Pear Sorbet (page 237).

Serves 6

700g ripe strawberries, hulled

juice of 1 lemon

½ quantity Sugar Syrup (see page 232, step 1)

100ml liquid glucose

1 Using the back of a spoon, push the strawberries through a sieve into a bowl. Stir in the lemon juice, sugar syrup and glucose.

2 When cold, transfer the mixture to an ice cream machine and churn until a soft sorbet has formed (about 30–45 minutes). If making by hand, see the tip on page 222.

LEMON SORBET

The simplest sorbet of all, this will go with absolutely everything.

Serves 6

600ml fresh lemon juice

1 quantity Sugar Syrup (see page 232, step 1)

1 Stir the lemon juice into the syrup, then set aside to cool.

2 When cold, transfer the mixture to an ice cream machine and churn until a soft sorbet has formed (about 30–45 minutes). If making by hand, see the tip on page 222.

lemon sorbet variation

Basil and Lemon Sorbet – put 190g caster sugar, 15g skimmed powdered milk and 100g liquid glucose into a saucepan. Add 300ml water and mix well over the heat until boiling. Take off the heat and add 100ml water, 300ml fresh lemon juice and a large handful of basil leaves. Cover and chill for about 12 hours. Whiz briefly in a blender (not too long, or it will turn grey), then strain through a fine sieve. Transfer to an ice cream machine and churn for about 45 minutes. If making by hand, see the tip on page 222.

APPLE SORBET WITH BLACKBERRY SAUCE

This sorbet is the taste of autumn. I like to include a cinnamon stick with the apples.

Serves 4

1 quantity Sugar Syrup (see page 232, step 1)

4 apples, peeled, cored and diced

1 cinnamon stick

grated zest and juice of 2 limes

For the sauce:

grated zest and juice of 1 orange

1 tablespoon crème de cassis liqueur

35g caster sugar

80g fresh blackberries

1 First make the sauce. Put the orange zest and juice, crème de cassis and sugar in a saucepan, bring to the boil and boil for 5 minutes. Add the blackberries, bring to a simmer and cook for a few minutes, then set aside.

2 Put the sugar syrup in a saucepan, add the apples, cinnamon and lime zest and juice and simmer until tender. Discard the cinnamon stick, then whiz the mixture until smooth. Set aside to cool.

3 When cold, transfer the mixture to an ice cream machine and churn until a soft sorbet has formed (about 30–45 minutes). If making by hand, see the tip on page 222.

4 To serve, place 2 scoops in a glass and dribble a little of the blackberry sauce over the top.

CUCUMBER AND LIME SORBET

A remarkably refreshing sorbet, delicious served on a summer's afternoon.

Serves 4

2 cucumbers, plus extra slices for decoration

300g plain yoghurt, plus extra for decoration

juice of 3 limes, strained

2 quantities Sugar Syrup (see page 232, step 1)

1 Peel the cucumbers, whiz the flesh in a blender – you need 700ml of the pulp – then push it through a fine sieve.

2 Stir the cucumber pulp, yoghurt and lime juice into the sugar syrup, then cover and chill for 24 hours.

3 Transfer the chilled mixture to an ice cream machine and churn until a soft sorbet has formed (about 30–45 minutes). If making by hand, see the tip on page 222.

4 To serve, top with a little extra yoghurt and cucumber slices.

FENNEL AND LIME SORBET

Another very refreshing sorbet. The colour is quite pale, but if you would like a distinctive green shade, add a drop of green food colouring.

Serves 4

1 fennel bulb, chopped

juice of 2 limes

150g caster sugar

450ml water

50ml pastis (aniseed-flavoured aperitif)

1 Place the fennel and lime juice in a saucepan, add the sugar and water and bring to the boil. Simmer for 15 minutes, then set aside to infuse for 4 hours.

2 Push the fennel mixture through a very fine sieve, then stir in the pastis.

3 Place the mixture in an ice cream machine and churn until a soft sorbet has formed (about 30–45 minutes). If making by hand, see the tip on page 222.

BEETROOT SORBET

This makes a wonderful starter. Serve it with some bitter salad leaves, such as rocket or mizuna, or a salty meat like bresaola.

Serves 6

300g cranberry juice

240g liquid glucose

300g caster sugar

800g cooked beetroot

1 Place the cranberry juice, liquid glucose and sugar in a saucepan. Bring to the boil, then set aside to cool.

2 Meanwhile, whiz the beetroot to a purée and pass it through a fine sieve.

3 Add the cooled cranberry mixture to the beetroot purée, then transfer to an ice cream machine and churn for about 45 minutes. If making by hand, see the tip on page 222.

FRUIT PUDDINGS

Fruit puddings should celebrate fruit in season
— or in winter, when there is no local fruit, the
best of the tropical fruits, such as pineapples,
mangoes and passion fruit. It's lovely to follow
the seasons, moving from the first forced rhubarb
through to summer berries, peaches and plums,
then apples, pears and quinces. And, of course,
we have citrus fruit available all year round for
desserts such as Lemon Posset (see page 250)
and Orange and Mint Jelly (page 245).

If you make jelly at home, you will be able to enjoy all the wonderful pure flavours of the fruit. The sabayon is a delicious way to finish this jelly for a special meal, but it's also very good served plain.

RED FRUIT JELLY

with Basil and Sauternes Sabayon

To make the jelly follow steps 1 to 5
To make the sabayon follow steps 9 to 11

SERVES 4

250g ripe strawberries, hulled

250g caster sugar

400ml boiling water

18g gelatine leaves

250g fresh raspberries

FOR THE SABAYON:

3 egg yolks

40g caster sugar

150ml Sauternes wine

1 tablespoon torn basil leaves

FOR DECORATION:

small bunches of redcurrants

basil leaves

1 Put the strawberries and sugar into a heatproof bowl and pour the boiling water over them.

2 Cover and set aside to infuse, stirring gently from time to time. After 1½ hours, pour half the strawberry liquid into a saucepan and heat until boiling.

3 Meanwhile, soak the gelatine in cold water for 15 minutes, then squeeze it dry.

4 Add it to the hot strawberry liquid off the heat and stir until dissolved. Strain into a bowl and set aside to cool.

5 When the strawberries have been sitting for a total of 2 hours, strain their remaining juice through a sieve into the gelatine mixture.

6 Reserve the strawberries for later.

7 Divide the raspberries between 4 glass tumblers and add just enough strawberry jelly to cover. Place in the fridge to set.

8 Top with the reserved strawberries and pour in the remaining jelly to come 1cm below the rim of the glasses. Return to the fridge to set.

9 To make the sabayon, put the egg yolks and sugar in a heatproof bowl set over a saucepan of simmering water and whisk until very pale.

10 Keep whisking while adding the wine, and continue whisking until the mixture holds its shape.

11 Take off the heat and whisk until it becomes cool. Fold in the torn basil leaves.

12 To serve, spoon the basil sabayon over each jelly, then decorate with redcurrants and basil leaves.

TIPS AND IDEAS

■ Pouring boiling water over the strawberries and sugar ensures the flavour comes out immediately. Be aware, though, that other fruits, such as raspberries, can't be steeped in the same way.

■ Be sure to use seasonal English strawberries for the jelly. They invariably have the best flavour.

■ Make sure the liquid is hot enough to melt the gelatine, but don't let it boil after adding the gelatine or it will become stringy.

■ If you are layering fruit in the jelly, pour a layer of jelly into each glass and let it set before adding the fruit, otherwise the fruit will sink to the bottom.

■ When making jelly, I always find it easier to use individual dishes rather than one big one. If you make it in glasses, as in this recipe, you won't need to go through the slightly nerve-racking process of turning it out.

■ If you do want to make one large jelly and turn it out, dip the base of the mould into warm water for a few seconds first. On a very hot day, the warmth of your hands might be enough to loosen it. I recommend metal jelly moulds – the jelly will turn out much more easily.

■ Little shot glasses of jelly are wonderful served with desserts – try elderflower jelly served with a lemon tart or raspberry jelly with a raspberry mousse.

■ When making the sabayon, do keep whisking until it's completely cold, otherwise it can separate.

■ Whisking the sabayon with a balloon whisk gives it slightly more volume. An electric whisk is easier, though!

ORANGE AND MINT JELLY

This is effectively a winter version of the recipe on page 242. It is delicious with the sabayon, but very refreshing without.

Serves 4

400ml fresh orange juice, strained

9g gelatine leaves

200ml water

100g caster sugar

2 tablespoons Grand Marnier liqueur (optional)

3 oranges

20 mint leaves, plus extra for decoration

1 quantity Sabayon, made with mint rather than basil (see pages 242–243, steps 9–11)

1 Pour half the orange juice into a bowl and soak the gelatine in it for 15 minutes.

2 Meanwhile, put the water and sugar into a saucepan and bring to a simmer. Take off the heat, add the gelatine and its soaking liquid and mix well until the gelatine has completely dissolved. Add the Grand Marnier (if using) and the remaining orange juice, mix well and set aside to cool.

3 Peel and segment the oranges, making sure all the pith is removed. Divide the segments and mint leaves between 4 pretty glass tumblers, and pour in just enough jelly to cover them. If your glasses are quite large, you don't have to fill them up.

4 Top with the mint sabayon decorated with extra mint leaves, and serve with Shortbread fingers (see page 173).

PEARS WITH GINGER JELLY

This is a great autumn/winter jelly. I like to serve it as a decoration for caramelised pears, as in this recipe, but it is also very good with apples or even Warm Chocolate Cakes (see page 73).

Serves 4

30g unsalted butter

75g caster sugar

3 large pears, peeled, cored and thinly sliced

40ml Poire William liqueur

1 teaspoon ground ginger

For the ginger jelly:

15g gelatine leaves

400ml Fentiman's Ginger Beer

25g caster sugar

1 First make the jelly. Soak the gelatine in cold water for 15 minutes, then squeeze dry. Whisk the ginger beer until the bubbles have gone, then pour it into a saucepan and bring to the boil with the sugar. Take off the heat, add the squeezed gelatine and stir until melted. Cool slightly, then pour into a gratin dish lined with cling film and chill for about 4 hours, until set.

2 Melt the butter and sugar in a large frying pan until you have a pale caramel. Add the pears and cook for 3 minutes. Add the Poire William and ginger and heat until the liquid is reduced to a syrup.

3 Invert the jelly on to a chopping board and peel off the cling film. Cut the jelly into 4 squares, place on serving plates and serve the pears alongside.

STRAWBERRY AND PINK CHAMPAGNE TERRINE WITH GINGER CHANTILLY CREAM

This is a celebration dish that uses one of my favourite ingredients – ginger. You might have noticed it cropping up rather a lot in this book. I make the terrine in 2 small loaf tins, which is easier, but you could use one large tin if you prefer. Cava or Prosecco makes a good substitute for Champagne if necessary.

Serves 8

30g gelatine leaves

500ml water

300g granulated sugar

600ml pink Champagne

sunflower oil for greasing

500g ripe small strawberries, hulled (larger ones can also be cut in half)

250g fresh raspberries

For the ginger Chantilly cream:

275g double cream

6 tablespoons syrup from a jar of stem ginger

1 Soak the gelatine in a little cold water for 15 minutes.

2 Meanwhile, put the water and sugar into a saucepan and bring to a simmer. Squeeze the gelatine dry and add it to the syrup, stirring well to make sure it is dissolved.

3 Pour the Champagne into a large bowl, add the syrup and mix well.

4 Lightly grease a two 450g loaf tins and line them with cling film, allowing it to overhang the edges.

5 Pour a 5mm depth of the Champagne jelly into the tins and let it set. Arrange half the strawberries on it, leaving a 1cm channel around the edges. Pour more jelly over them and place in the freezer for 20 minutes.

6 Arrange all the raspberries over the other layers, again leaving a 1cm channel around the edges. Cover with more jelly and freeze for another 20 minutes.

7 Add a final layer of strawberries and jelly, then set in the fridge overnight.

8 To make the ginger Chantilly cream, whisk the cream into soft peaks. Whisk in the stem ginger syrup a bit at a time, whisking lightly so that the mixture does not separate. Cover and store in the fridge until needed.

9 To serve, dip the bases of the terrines into boiling water for 10 seconds, then invert on to a plate. Cut into slices 1.5cm thick and serve with the Chantilly cream.

RASPBERRY AND RUM TRIFLE

Making this in individual glasses means you don't have to serve it out yourself, but it does look quite spectacular made in one large bowl if you want to give it a go.

Serves 4

4 tablespoons rum

200ml double cream

toasted flaked almonds

For the sponge base:

100g ground almonds

100g caster sugar

1 egg, plus 1 egg yolk

25g soft unsalted butter

20g plain flour

3 egg whites

For the jelly:

6g gelatine leaves

700g frozen raspberries

icing sugar, to taste

2 tablespoons boiling water

For the custard:

500ml double cream

2 vanilla pods, split open lengthways

10 egg yolks

80g caster sugar

---

trifle variation

Cherry Trifle – prepare the sponge circles as above, but sprinkle with sherry rather than rum. Cover with black cherry jam, then top with the custard as before and a layer of Chantilly Cream (see Strawberry and Chantilly Cream Swiss Roll, page 78). Decorate each serving with a black cherry and chopped pistachios.

---

1 First make the sponge base. Put the ground almonds, caster sugar, whole egg and egg yolk, butter and flour in a large bowl and stir together. Whisk the egg whites to soft peaks. Using a metal spoon, fold 2 tablespoons of the whites into the almond mixture, then gently fold in the rest. Do not beat.

2 Pour the mixture on a baking sheet lined with baking parchment and bake in the centre of an oven preheated to 180°C/Gas Mark 4 for 10 minutes, until golden brown. Set aside to cool on the parchment.

3 Using a pastry cutter, stamp out circles of the sponge and use to line the bottom of 4 large wineglasses. Drizzle a tablespoon of rum over each one and leave to soak in.

4 To make the jelly, soak the gelatine in cold water for 15 minutes, then squeeze dry. Meanwhile, set aside a dozen of the best-looking raspberries. Rub the remainder through a sieve to make a thick juice. Sift in enough icing sugar to sweeten. Put the squeezed gelatine in a bowl with the boiling water. Stir to dissolve, then add to the raspberry juice. Mix well and pour evenly over each glass of sponge. Place in the fridge to set.

5 To make the custard, put the cream and the seeds scraped from the vanilla pods in a saucepan and bring to a simmer. Put the egg yolks and sugar in a bowl and whisk until the sugar has dissolved. Whisk in the hot cream, then return the mixture to the saucepan, bring to the boil and stir until it thickens. Cover with cling film, placing it directly on top of the custard to prevent a skin forming, and set aside to cool.

6 Pour a thick layer of the custard into each trifle glass. Whip the 200ml cream until stiff, then pipe or spoon some into each glass. Decorate with the reserved raspberries and the flaked almonds.

GINGER ELDERFLOWER SYLLABUB

This is another storecupboard dessert, and it's very quick to make. If you're in a rush you don't even have to chill it — just whisk it and serve straight away.

Serves 4

50ml Elderflower and Lemon Cordial (see page 276)

50ml syrup from a jar of stem ginger

50g caster sugar

280ml double cream

zest of 1 lemon

2 tablespoons crushed pistachios for sprinkling

1 Put the cordial, stem ginger syrup and sugar into a saucepan and bring to a simmer. Once the sugar has dissolved, set aside to get cold.

2 Whip the cream to soft peaks. Slowly whisk in the cooled syrup and the lemon zest. Spoon or pipe the mixture into 4 serving glasses, then chill for 2–3 hours. Sprinkle with crushed pistachios before serving.

LEMON POSSET

This is probably the easiest dish in the whole book — just three ingredients and 5 minutes to prepare. It's also one of the most delicious. Forget the calories and just do it.

Serves 6

600ml double cream

140g caster sugar

grated zest and juice of 2 large lemons

1 Put the cream and sugar into a saucepan, bring slowly to the boil, then simmer for 3 minutes. Take off the heat, add the lemon zest and juice and whisk well.

2 Pour the mixture into 6 small ramekins and chill for 2–3 hours, until set.

RED BERRY FRUIT SALAD

The quintessential summer fruit salad. You can omit the sugar if you like, but a little bit goes a long way in this case.

Serves 6

150g ripe strawberries, hulled and halved or quartered, depending on size

150g fresh blackcurrants, topped and tailed

150g fresh redcurrants, stalks removed

150g fresh loganberries

150g fresh raspberries

juice of ½ lime

juice of 1 orange

50g caster sugar

1 Put all the berries into a bowl with the citrus juice and sugar. Mix well but carefully to avoid crushing the fruit.

2 Spoon into individual glasses and serve with Chantilly Cream (see Strawberry and Chantilly Cream Swiss Roll, page 78).

SUMMER PUDDING

Summer on a plate. It's not traditional, but I like to include peaches. Don't over-soak the bread or it will fall apart.

Serves 6

6g gelatine leaves

100ml water

juice of 1 lemon

200g caster sugar

30ml elderflower cordial

1kg prepared mixed ripe red fruit, e.g. strawberries, raspberries, redcurrants, blackcurrants

200g ripe peaches, halved, stoned and skinned (see page 260, step 1) and finely sliced

8–10 slices of white bread, 1 or 2 days old, crusts removed

1 Soak the gelatine leaves in cold water for 15 minutes, then squeeze dry.

2 Meanwhile, put the water, lemon juice, sugar and elderflower cordial into a saucepan and heat gently until the sugar has dissolved. Add all the fruit, bring to the boil and simmer for 1 minute. Take off the heat, add the squeezed-out gelatine and mix carefully so as not to crush the fruit. Set aside to cool for a little while.

3 Strain the fruit juice into a shallow bowl and soak one side of the bread slices in it. Use the bread to line a 1kg pudding basin, soaked-side out, but save enough to use as a lid.

4 Fill the lined basin with the fruit, cover with the remaining bread and put a small plate and a heavy weight on top. Place in the fridge overnight.

5 Turn the pudding on to a dish and serve with thick double cream.

CHILLED MELON SOUP

This is the simplest of fruit soups and has lovely, clean flavours. The melons need to be very ripe indeed. I like to use Cantaloupe (or Charentais) melons for their colour, but other melons will be fine too.

Serves 4

2 very ripe cantaloupe melons

¼ watermelon

juice of 1 lime

1 tablespoon raspberry vinegar

a pinch of salt

1 Deseed the melons and watermelon, cut the flesh from the skin and place in a blender. Add the lime juice, vinegar and salt, then whiz to a purée.

2 Push the purée through a fine sieve into a bowl and chill well before serving.

CHILLED RASPBERRY SOUP

A really refreshing alternative dessert. If you are lucky enough to grow your own raspberries, this is a wonderful way of using them up.

Serves 4

250ml sweet dessert wine

125ml red wine

250ml Champagne

100g caster sugar, plus 1 extra tablespoon (optional)

juice of ½ lemon

1 vanilla pod

450g fresh raspberries

10 whole mint leaves, plus 4 finely chopped

1 Put all the wine into a saucepan. Add the 100g sugar, lemon juice and whole vanilla pod, bring to the boil and boil for 3 minutes to remove the alcohol. Add 250g of the raspberries and set aside to cool for 5 minutes.

2 Remove the vanilla pod, then pour the contents of the pan into a blender and whiz to a purée. Transfer it to a bowl, add the whole mint leaves and leave to infuse in the fridge for at least 2 hours. When ice cold, push the purée through a fine sieve into a jug.

3 Put the remaining raspberries into a bowl, add the chopped mint and an extra tablespoon sugar (if you wish) and mix well. Place a spoonful of this mixture in each serving bowl and pour the soup around it.

Crème brûlée is a dessert that will never be out of fashion. It is one of the easiest you can make and quite versatile in terms of flavouring. This is a winter version with prunes, but you can dress it up with berries instead in the summer.

CRÈME BRÛLÉE

with Prunes and Armagnac

To make the crème brûlée, follow steps 3 to 9

SERVES 6

6 prunes, stoned

Armagnac for soaking

7 egg yolks

75g caster sugar, plus extra for sprinkling

600ml double cream

200ml whipping cream

1 vanilla pod, split open lengthways

1 Put the prunes in bowl, cover with Armagnac and set aside to soak overnight, or for at least 4 hours.

2 After that, cut each prune in half and place in six small ramekins.

3 Put the egg yolks and sugar in a bowl and whisk until light.

4 Pour both creams into a saucepan, scrape in the seeds from the vanilla pod and add the pod, then bring to the boil.

5 Discard the vanilla pod and add the hot cream to the egg yolk mixture, whisking all the time.

6 Pour it into a jug and fill the ramekins to the top.

7 Place them in a baking tin and add enough cold water to come three-quarters of the way up the dishes.

8 Place in an oven preheated to 140°C/Gas Mark 1 for 2 hours, or until they are set. Remove the dishes and set aside to cool.

9 Sprinkle a thin layer of sugar over each ramekin, then caramelise it with a blowtorch or under a hot grill.

TIPS AND IDEAS

■ You can keep the crème brûlée in the fridge for a couple of days before caramelising and then just caramelise it shortly before serving. Don't put it in the fridge after caramelising the top, though, or the topping will become soggy.

■ I use a mixture of double and whipping cream to prevent the crème brûlée being too heavy.

■ Don't be tempted to turn the oven up; the crème brûlée is better cooked very slowly so that there is no risk of it curdling or going grainy.

■ The crème brûlée is ready when it is just set but still has a slight wobble in the centre; as it cools, it will firm up a little more.

■ Crème brûlée can also be cooked in shallow dishes, such as eared dishes, in which case it will need a little less time in the oven.

■ The trick to caramelising it properly is to make sure the sugar is just a thin layer. I put the ramekin on a plate and scatter the sugar on top so that the excess sugar falls on the plate and can be re-used. Then I transfer the crème brûlée to another plate to blowtorch it.

■ Don't put the blowtorch too close to the sugar – about 7cm should do. When the sugar just begins to caramelise, move the blowtorch to the next spot. Keep moving it until you have worked all over the dessert.

■ A word of warning: don't touch the hot sugar. It will burn you very badly indeed.

■ Once the desserts have been caramelised, leave for a few minutes until the top is hard and crisp. Diners should be able to tap it lightly with the back of their spoon to crack the caramel.

■ To make a coffee version, bring the cream to the boil with a handful of coffee beans, then remove from the heat and leave overnight. Strain and reheat gently. Star anise, cinnamon stick, cardamom seeds and even black peppercorns also work well like this.

COCONUT RICE PUDDING WITH PEACH SAUCE

Coconut milk provides a little twist in this rice pudding. It is cooked on the stove instead of in the oven and can be prepared the day before if necessary, since it is eaten chilled. Mango or pineapple would work well instead of peach.

Serves 8

125g short grain pudding rice

300ml coconut milk

200ml full-fat milk

100g caster sugar

200ml double cream, lightly whipped

For the sauce:

2 Poached Peaches (see page 272)

juice of 1 lemon

½ quantity Sugar Syrup (see page 232, step 1)

1 Put the rice, coconut milk, milk and sugar in a heavy-based pan, bring to a simmer and cook gently, stirring constantly, for about 35 minutes, until the rice is tender. Cover with cling film, placing it directly on top of the rice to prevent a skin forming, and set aside until cold and thickened.

2 Just before serving, stir in the cream. Place six 5cm mousse rings on a tray and fill to the brim with the rice. Set in the fridge for 2–3 hours, or overnight if you want to prepare the pudding well in advance.

3 Meanwhile, make the sauce. Put the peaches into a blender, add the lemon juice and whiz to a purée. Pour into a jug and stir in the sugar syrup.

4 Turn the rice out of the rings into shallow bowls and pour some of the peach sauce around them.

BAKED APPLES WITH RUM-SOAKED RAISINS

The rum lifts this nursery pudding to a new level. You could, of course, soak the raisins in apple juice instead if you like.

Serves 4

100g raisins

100ml rum

4 large Bramley apples

100g soft dark brown sugar

100g soft unsalted butter

½ teaspoon ground cinnamon

1 Put the raisins into a bowl, cover with the rum and set aside to soak for 2 hours.

2 Using a small thin knife, peel and core the apples, keeping the fruit whole. Place them in a shallow baking tin.

3 Place the sugar in a bowl with the rum and raisins, half the butter and the cinnamon and mix well.

4 Press the raisin mixture into the centre of each apple, put a knob of the remaining butter on top and bake in an oven preheated to 180°C/Gas Mark 4 for about 40 minutes, until soft. Serve with cream or ice cream.

BAKED APPLES WITH HAZELNUTS

Cox's Orange Pippins work well, here but any well-flavoured eating apples will do. Using eating apples means you need less sugar, as they are naturally sweet.

Serves 8

8 large eating apples

75g soft light brown sugar

75g raisins

75g soft unsalted butter

½ teaspoon ground ginger

50g hazelnuts, crushed

1 Using a small thin knife, peel and core the apples, keeping the fruit whole. Place them in a shallow baking tin.

2 Put the sugar into a bowl, add the raisins, half the butter, the ginger and hazelnuts and mix well.

3 Press the raisin mixture into the centre of each apple, put a knob of the remaining butter on top and bake in an oven preheated to 180°C/Gas Mark 4 for about 30 minutes, until soft. Serve with cream or ice cream.

BAKED PEACHES WITH AMARETTO

One of the simplest and best dishes to make when peaches are in season. Peach and almond are natural partners.

Serves 4

6 peaches, halved and stoned

unsalted butter for greasing

2 tablespoons sugar mixed with seeds from 1 vanilla pod

6 small amaretti biscuits, crushed

150ml Amaretto liqueur

1 Lightly score a cross on the base of each peach. Put them in a pan of boiling water for 20 seconds, then transfer to a bowl of iced water. Remove the peaches from the bowl and carefully peel off the skin.

2 Place the peaches in a buttered ovenproof dish, cut-side up. Sprinkle the sugar and amaretti over them, then pour the Amaretto around them.

3 Bake in an oven preheated to 180°C/Gas Mark 4 for 15 minutes. Serve warm with whipped cream.

BAKED PEARS WITH ORANGE AND ALMOND

This recipe is really easy to make and ideal for when you need to rustle up a pudding in a hurry. It's delicious served with a dollop of crème fraîche or double cream.

Serves 4

4 pears, just about ripe

100g unsalted butter, plus extra for greasing

75g soft dark brown sugar

75g granulated sugar

juice of 2 oranges

1 tablespoon fresh lemon juice

100ml dessert wine or water

2 teaspoons raspberry vinegar

100g flaked almonds

1 Peel the pears, cut them in half lengthways and remove the core.

2 Generously butter a large baking dish and arrange the pears in it flat-side down.

3 Put the butter, sugars, citrus juices, wine or water and vinegar in a saucepan. Heat, stirring, until dissolved. Pour this syrup over the pears.

4 Cover the dish with foil and bake in an oven preheated to 180°C/Gas Mark 4 for 20 minutes, basting a couple of times. Remove the foil, sprinkle the almonds over the fruit and bake for another 10 minutes. Serve warm with double cream.

APPLE CRUMBLE

Perfect as it is, but also delicious with other fruits added, such as rhubarb, blackberries or raspberries.

Serves 4–6

900g apples, peeled, cored and cut into 1cm pieces

100g unrefined brown sugar

2 pinches of ground cinnamon

For the crumble:

300g plain flour, sifted

a pinch of salt

150g unrefined brown sugar

50g caster sugar

175g unsalted butter, cut into small pieces, plus extra for greasing

zest of 2 oranges

zest of 2 lemons

1 First make the crumble. Place the flour, salt and sugars in a large bowl and mix well. Taking a few pieces of butter at a time, rub them into the flour mixture until it resembles breadcrumbs. Add the zest of 1 orange and 1 lemon.

2 Place the apples in a large bowl and sprinkle over the brown sugar, cinnamon and remaining orange and lemon zest. Stir well, being careful not to break up the fruit.

3 Spoon the fruit mixture into a buttered 23cm ovenproof dish, then sprinkle the crumble over the top. Bake in an oven preheated to 180°C/Gas Mark 4 for 40–45 minutes, until the crumble is browned and the fruit mixture bubbling. Serve with thick cream or custard.

RHUBARB CRUMBLE

The porridge oats and hazelnuts give this crumble a rustic feel – I first had it in Scotland, naturally!

Serves 4

800g forced rhubarb, cut into 2cm lengths

200g caster sugar

40g unsalted butter, melted, plus extra for greasing

grated zest and juice of 1 orange

juice of ½ lemon

For the crumble:

175g cold unsalted butter, cut into small pieces

200g plain flour

100g porridge oats

150g soft light brown sugar

50g hazelnuts

1 Place the rhubarb in a 23cm buttered baking dish. Sprinkle the sugar, butter, orange zest and juices over it.

2 To make the crumble, put the butter and flour into a food processor or bowl and pulse or rub together until the mixture resembles fine breadcrumbs. Add the oats and sugar and pulse or stir for just 5 seconds. Add the hazelnuts and pulse or stir again for 2 seconds.

3 Sprinkle the crumble evenly over the rhubarb. Bake in an oven preheated to 180°C/Gas Mark 4 for about 45 minutes, until a golden crust forms.

SYRUPS
CORDIALS and
COMPOTES

This chapter includes an irresistible selection of fruit in flavoured syrups. Once you have made a simple sugar syrup, it is very easy to flavour it and use it for poaching fruit. You can also use flavoured syrups in sorbets or fruit salads – they are incredibly useful things to keep in the fridge. Cordials are a very cheap way of making your own drinks. Elderflower cordial is one of the best – and you can pick the main ingredient for free.

This autumnal dish has a wonderfully subtle aniseed note from the star anise. It makes a delicious dessert, but you can also serve it as an accompaniment to game, such as venison, or even duck.

PEARS IN ANISEED SYRUP

To poach the pears follow steps 1 to 6

SERVES 4

2 quantities Sugar Syrup (see page 232, step 1)

2 strips of orange zest

4 star anise

4 pears, just about ripe

1 Put all the ingredients apart from the pears into a saucepan large enough to hold the fruit.

2 Bring to the boil, then simmer for about 15 minutes.

3 Meanwhile, carefully peel the pears, keeping them whole and with the stalks on.

4 Using a thin, sharp knife, carefully remove the cores from the calyx end.

5 Add the pears to the pan, ensuring they are submerged in the syrup.

6 Place a circle of greaseproof paper directly over the fruit and simmer for 20 minutes. Set aside to cool.

7 When cold, use a slotted spoon to transfer the pears to a large serving bowl.

8 Pour the syrup into a saucepan and heat until reduced and thick.

9 Strain through a sieve, allow to cool, then pour the syrup over the pears.

TIPS AND IDEAS

■ The pears will keep for at least 3 days in the fridge.

■ Try to find pears that are only just ripe for this dish. I go for plump pears such as Comice – unless I am making this to serve as a garnish for meat dishes, in which case I use slender varieties such as Conference.

■ It's a good idea to cut a thin sliver from the base of each pear so that it will stand up straight.

■ If you don't have a deep enough pan, you can cut the pears in half before cooking them. A little trick is to cut the stalk in half and then cut down through the pear so that each half has its own stalk – then simply remove the core. Halved pears will take a little less time to cook.

■ The circle of greaseproof paper helps to keep the pears submerged in the liquid. The technical name for it is a cartouche.

■ You need to reduce the syrup until it is thick enough to coat the pears lightly, but remember that it will thicken further as it cools.

■ I like to let the pears cool in the syrup after cooking so that they become infused with the flavour of the star anise.

■ After the pears have cooled, you can fill the cavity with chocolate ganache (see Chocolate Swiss Roll, page 78) or ice cream (see page 220), if you like.

■ A flavoured syrup is a building block of a recipe, rather than a whole dish. You can use it in various ways – my favourite is to add a little to a glass of Champagne.

syrup variations

Ginger Syrup – omit the orange zest and star anise and add a 7.5cm piece of finely diced fresh ginger and the grated zest and juice of 2 lemons to the sugar syrup, as on page 265, step 1. Bring to the boil, then simmer for 2 minutes, until slightly thickened. Set aside to infuse for 24 hours. Strain and store in sterilised bottles (see page 274). The syrup will keep for ages.

Spiced Ginger Syrup with Lemongrass – omit the orange zest; crush the star anise and add to the simmering syrup along with 2 teaspoons crushed allspice berries, 4 whole cloves and 2 crushed lemongrass stalks, as on page 265, step 2. Strain and store in sterilised bottles (see page 274).

Lavender and Vanilla Syrup – omit the orange zest and star anise. Add 2 teaspoons vanilla extract and a big handful of lavender flowers to the sugar syrup as on page 265, step 1. Bring to the boil and simmer for 2 minutes. Set aside to infuse for 4 hours. Strain and store in sterilised bottles (see page 274).

PEARS IN RED WINE AND ROSEMARY SYRUP

You cannot go wrong with pears in red wine. Serve with vanilla ice cream – the contrast between the rich, dark syrup and pale ice cream is beautiful.

Serves 4

1 bottle of good red wine

250g caster sugar

2 strips of orange rind, most of pith sliced off

juice of 1 lemon

1 large sprig of rosemary

4 pears, just about ripe

1 Put all the ingredients apart from the pears into a large saucepan, bring to the boil, then simmer for about 15 minutes.

2 Meanwhile, carefully peel the pears, keeping them whole and with the stalks on.

3 Add the peeled pears to the pan, place a circle of greaseproof paper directly over the fruit and simmer for 20 minutes. Set aside to cool.

4 When cold, use a slotted spoon to transfer the pears to a large serving bowl. Pour the syrup into a saucepan and heat until reduced and thick. Strain through a sieve, allow to cool, then pour the syrup over the pears.

AUTUMN FRUIT IN ROSEMARY SYRUP

Rosemary is an extraordinary herb to use here. It is so fragrant and gives off a beguiling aroma when added to sweet things.

Serves 4

100g caster sugar

50g light muscovado sugar

250ml water

grated zest and juice of 2 lemons

4 small sprigs of rosemary

6 plums, halved and stoned

300g ripe blackberries

1 Put the sugars and water in a saucepan and heat gently, stirring until the sugars have dissolved. Bring to the boil and simmer for 10 minutes.

2 Add the lemon zest and juice, rosemary and plums and bring back to a simmer. Poach the plums gently until they are just tender.

3 Take the pan off the heat, discard the rosemary and stir in the blackberries. Serve lukewarm with vanilla ice cream.

POACHED FIGS WITH STAR ANISE

Fresh figs cope well with robust flavours such as port and red wine. Do be careful not to overcook them, though – if they are properly ripe they will need only a couple of minutes.

Serves 6

150g caster sugar

150ml port

150ml red wine

8 star anise

2 cloves

400ml water

12 fresh figs

1 Put all the ingredients apart from the figs into a saucepan big enough to hold the figs quite snugly upright. Bring to the boil and boil for 1 minute

2 Add the figs and cook over a medium heat for 2–3 minutes. Set the pan aside to cool.

3 Transfer the cooled figs to a shallow serving dish, then return the pan to the heat and reduce the syrup until it is slightly thicker. Strain the syrup through a sieve, allow to cool and thicken a little more, then pour over the figs.

POACHED QUINCES

This simple dish is the perfect way to cook peaches in season. I like to use white peaches.

Serves 6

1.75 litres water

200g caster sugar

1 lemon, cut in half

1 vanilla pod, split open lengthways

700g quinces, peeled, quartered and cored

1 Put the water, sugar, lemon and seeds scraped from the vanilla pod into a saucepan and bring to a simmer.

2 Add the vanilla pod and quinces, cover and cook for about 1½ hours, or until a sharp knife goes in easily; some varieties of quince may take twice as long. Set the pan aside to cool.

3 Transfer the cooled quinces to a shallow serving dish, then return the pan to the heat and, if necessary, reduce the syrup until it is slightly thicker. Cool, strain and pour over the quinces.

CLEMENTINES AND CANDIED PEEL POACHED IN SAUTERNES

This makes a delicious alternative Christmas dessert. Homemade candied peel has a much fresher flavour than the bought stuff. Be aware that it doesn't keep as well, though.

Serves 6

zest of 2 oranges, cut into fine strips

300g caster sugar, plus extra for rolling

225ml water

6 seedless clementines, peeled but left whole

ground cinnamon, to taste

200ml Sauternes wine

100ml Grand Marnier liqueur

1 Put the orange zest into boiling water for 15 seconds, then refresh under cold water. Return to clean boiling water for 2 minutes, then refresh again.

2 Put the sugar and water into a high-rimmed sauté pan and bring to a simmer. Add the orange zest and simmer for 5 minutes. Add the clementines and simmer for a further 5 minutes. Using a slotted spoon, transfer them to a shallow serving dish and set aside.

3 Continue to simmer the orange zest for about 15–20 minutes, until it has a sticky consistency. Meanwhile, cover a sheet of waxed paper with a thick layer of sugar.

4 Using a slotted spoon, remove the zest from the pan and separate the strips. Roll them in the sugar, adding cinnamon to taste, then transfer to a plate. They should keep for a couple of weeks in the fridge.

5 Add the Sauternes and Grand Marnier to the sugar syrup and heat to reduce a little, taking care as the alcohol may ignite. Return the clementines to the pan and cook for 5 minutes, turning them once.

6 Using a slotted spoon, transfer the clementines to a serving dish. Reduce the liquid in the pan to a syrup consistency, then pour over the fruit and top with some of the candied peel.

POACHED PEACHES

This simple dish is the perfect way to cook peaches in season. I like to use white peaches.

Serves 4

4 ripe peaches

350ml water

130g caster sugar

grated zest and juice of 2 lemons

1 Cut a few little incisions into the skin of the peaches. Place the fruit in a saucepan of boiling water and boil for 30 seconds. Remove with a slotted spoon and peel off the skin.

2 Add the sugar and lemon zest to the water, bring to the boil, then simmer for a few minutes. Add the lemon juice and poach the peaches in the simmering syrup for 5 minutes. If your peaches aren't quite as ripe as you'd like, simmer them for a further 5 minutes, or until soft. Set aside until cold.

CHERRIES IN RED WINE

A light, fruity wine is good for this. Delicious served with pistachio ice cream.

Serves 6

700ml red wine

260g caster sugar

1kg fresh cherries, stoned

1 Put the wine and sugar into a saucepan and bring to the boil. Add the cherries and simmer for 1 minute. Strain the cherries into a heatproof bowl, then return the liquid to the heat and reduce it to a light syrup.

2 Pour the syrup over the cherries, then set aside to cool. Cover and chill until required.

cherries in red wine variation

Plums in Red Wine – put 200g caster sugar and 400ml red wine into a saucepan, bring to the boil, then simmer for about 5 minutes to make a syrup. Add 8 whole red plums, stems removed, to the saucepan, topping up the syrup with water if they are not quite covered. Poach gently for 10 minutes. Using a slotted spoon, transfer the plums to a bowl, then boil the syrup to reduce by one-third. Pour the syrup over the plums and set aside to cool.

SPICED CHERRIES

This can be served simply as a dessert but is also very good as a filling for little tarts, on a base of crème pâtissière (see page 120).

Serves 6

2 star anise

1 teaspoon ground allspice

14cm cinnamon stick

200g caster sugar

2 strips of orange rind, most of pith sliced off

½ bottle of red wine

juice of 1 lemon

1kg fresh cherries, stoned

1 Put all the ingredients, apart from the cherries, into a saucepan and bring to the boil.

2 Add the cherries and simmer for about 10 minutes, until tender. Set aside to cool in the pan.

3 Strain the cherries into a bowl, then return the liquid to heat and reduce a syrup. Set aside to cool, then pour over the fruit.

SPICED ORANGES AND SULTANAS

A simple and delicious winter fruit salad. You could substitute a vanilla pod for the cinnamon stick and allspice.

Serves 4

120g caster sugar

120ml water

120g sultanas

2 tablespoons fresh lemon juice

1 cinnamon stick

½ teaspoon ground allspice

2 tablespoons crystallised ginger, very finely chopped

4 large oranges, segmented

1 Put the sugar and water into a small saucepan and bring to the boil. Add the sultanas, lemon juice, cinnamon stick, allspice and ginger and simmer over a medium heat for about 10 minutes, until the syrup has thickened. Set aside to cool.

2 Place the orange segments in a bowl, pour the cooled syrup over them, removing the cinnamon stick, and stir gently. Cover and chill for at least 2 hours. Serve with ice cream or cake.

BOTTLED PEARS

If you have a glut of pears in your garden, this is a lovely way to use them up. Bottling fruit in season means you have an instant product at your disposal throughout the rest of the year. I use these pears in so many ways: in a frangipane tart, served whole with ice cream or diced with panna cotta, for example (see page 210).

Makes six 500g jars

1½ teaspoons fine sea salt

2.5kg pears, just about ripe, peeled, halved and cored

1.5 litres water

750g caster sugar

juice of 2 lemons

1 Dissolve the salt in a bowl of water, add the pears and stir briefly. Rinse well and drain. Pack the pears into 6 sterilised 500g jars (see box below).

2 Put the water into a large saucepan, add the sugar and lemon juice and bring to the boil. Continue boiling until it reaches 60°C and becomes a syrup.

3 Pour the syrup into the jars of pears and sit the lids on top, not clipped or screwed down. Place the jars in a pan and pour water heated to 38°C around them. Gradually heat the pan until the water reaches 88°C, then maintain that temperature for 30 minutes.

4 Carefully remove the jars from the pan and tighten the lids. Label and date the jars, then store in a cool, dark place (a larder is ideal) for at least 3 weeks before eating.

ORANGE CORDIAL

I came to making cordials quite late and was surprised to see how simple it was. Adding citric acid to cordials increases the shelf life, but if you plan to drink it within a few days, you won't need it.

Makes 900ml

800ml water

800g caster sugar

juice of 1 lemon

4 large oranges

15g citric acid

1 Put the sugar and water into a saucepan, bring to the boil, then simmer for 2 minutes. Stir in the lemon juice.

2 Put the whole oranges into a blender or food processor and whiz to a purée. Add the citric acid and transfer to a heatproof bowl.

3 Pour in the simmering syrup and mix well. Cover with a clean tea towel and leave in a cool place for 24 hours.

4 Strain through a muslin-lined sieve and store in sterilised bottles (see box below). The cordial will keep for 3–4 months. To serve, dilute with water and add lots of ice.

to sterilise glass bottles and jars

To sterilise glass bottles and jars, wash them and their lids thoroughly in very hot water. Allow them to dry, then place in an oven preheated to 140°C/Gas Mark 1 for about 20 minutes. Remove and leave to cool for 10 minutes before filling them.

ELDERFLOWER AND LEMON CORDIAL

Elderflower has a very short season in early summer, so take advantage of it while you can. If you make a big batch of cordial, you can enjoy it throughout the year.

Makes 900ml

12 large elderflower heads

800ml water

800g caster sugar

grated zest and juice of 2 lemons

30g citric acid

1 Shake the elderflowers over a sheet of newspaper to get rid of any bugs. Place the flowers in a large heatproof bowl.

2 Put the water, sugar and lemon juice in a saucepan, bring to the boil and stir well until the sugar has dissolved. Add the lemon zest and citric acid and then stir again.

3 Pour the boiling syrup over the elderflowers, cover with a clean tea towel and leave in a cool place for 24 hours.

4 Strain through a muslin-lined sieve and store in sterilised bottles (see box, page 274). The cordial will keep for 3–4 months. To serve, dilute with water and add lots of ice.

GOOSEBERRY AND ELDERFLOWER CORDIAL

Gooseberries and elderflower just overlap, at the beginning of June. If you manage to find both, this is a lovely combination.

Makes 1.8 litres

14 elderflower heads

800ml water

1.2kg caster sugar

grated zest and juice of 1 lemon

1kg gooseberries, topped and tailed

35g citric acid

1 Shake the elderflowers over a sheet of newspaper to get rid of any bugs. Place the flowers in a large heatproof bowl.

2 Put the water, sugar and lemon juice into a saucepan, bring to the boil and stir well until the sugar has dissolved. Add the lemon zest and then stir again.

3 Add the gooseberries and simmer for a further 15 minutes.

4 Pour the boiling fruit and syrup over the elderflowers and add the citric acid. Cover with a clean tea towel and leave in a cool place for 24 hours.

5 Strain through a muslin-lined sieve and store in sterilised bottles (see box, page 274). The cordial will keep for 3–4 months. To serve, dilute with water and add lots of ice and mint leaves.

RED BERRY AND MINT CORDIAL

With its gorgeous colour, this makes an interesting alternative to shop-bought cordials. I use it as a sweetener in savoury sauces too.

Makes 1.8 litres

800g prepared mixed ripe red fruit e.g. blackcurrants, raspberries, strawberries, redcurrants

juice of 2 lemons

12 mint leaves

1 teaspoon tartaric acid

500ml water

500g caster sugar

1 Put the berries into a large heatproof bowl and add the lemon juice, mint and tartaric acid.

2 Put the water and sugar in a saucepan, bring to the boil and stir well until the sugar has dissolved.

3 Pour the boiling syrup over the berry mixture and stir well. Cover with a cloth and leave in a cool place (not the fridge) to infuse for 12 hours.

4 Strain through a muslin-lined sieve and store in sterilised bottles (see box, page 274). The cordial will keep for 3–4 months. To serve, dilute with water and add lots of ice and lovage flowers.

STRAWBERRY COMPOTE

The strawberries are barely cooked here, just heated until the juices run. The taste and aroma are the essence of summer.

Serves 4

400g ripe strawberries, hulled and quartered

200g caster sugar

1 Put the strawberries and sugar into a saucepan and heat until the juices start to run and the sugar has dissolved. Simmer for 1 minute. Set aside to cool. If covered and stored in the fridge, the compote will keep for 2–3 days.

FORCED RHUBARB AND GINGER COMPOTE

Forced rhubarb is available from January onwards and has a lovely delicate texture and flavour. Serve this compote with ice cream (see page 220) or panna cotta (see page 210).

Serves 4

100ml water

100g caster sugar

2cm piece of fresh ginger

500g forced rhubarb, cut into 2cm lengths

1 Put the water and sugar into a saucepan, bring to the boil and stir well until the sugar has dissolved. Simmer for 2 minutes, then take off the heat.

2 Peel the ginger and add just the skin to the syrup. Allow to infuse for 30 minutes, then strain through a fine sieve to remove the ginger skin.

3 Finely grate the ginger and add to the syrup along with the rhubarb. Bring to the boil for 1 minute, then set aside until cold. If covered and stored in the fridge, the compote will keep for 4–5 days.

RASPBERRY AND BLACKCURRANT COMPOTE

Serve this on its own or with ice cream, or strain off the juices and use the berries as a filling for tarts. It would also be lovely with Warm Chocolate Cakes (see page 73).

Serves 4

150ml water

150g caster sugar

150g fresh raspberries

150g fresh blackcurrants

100g fresh redcurrants, stalks removed

zest of 1 lemon

1 Put the water and sugar into a saucepan, bring to the boil and stir well until the sugar has dissolved. Simmer for 1 minute.

2 When the syrup has simmered for 1 minute, add all the fruit and the lemon zest. Simmer for 10 minutes, then set aside until cold. If covered and stored in the fridge, the compote will keep for 4–5 days.

APPLE COMPOTE

This is one of the most versatile compotes – delicious on its own, with yoghurt, in an apple tart or as an accompaniment to roast pork. Adding the butter is optional, but it does enrich it.

Serves 4

500g Cox's apples, peeled, cored and diced

100ml water

100g caster sugar

1 cinnamon stick

4 cloves

60g unsalted butter, cut into small pieces (optional)

1 Place the diced apples in a saucepan with the water and cook over a medium heat for 20 minutes, stirring occasionally.

2 Add the sugar, cinnamon and cloves and continue cooking on a low heat for 5 minutes.

3 Take off the heat and stir in the butter (if using). Set aside until cold. If covered and stored in the fridge, the compote will keep for 4–5 days.

STEWED FRUIT COMPOTE

At Christmas you can add various spices to this compote. Use cinnamon sticks, cloves, ginger or anything else that takes your fancy.

Serves 6

150g stoned prunes, soaked overnight

150g dried apricots

150g dried figs, stemmed (optional)

grates zest and strained juice of 1 orange

1 vanilla pod

100g caster sugar or honey

1 Put the prunes, apricots and figs (if using) into a medium saucepan. Add the remaining ingredients and enough water to cover, then bring to the boil and simmer for 10 minutes.

2 Set aside until cold. If covered and stored in the fridge, the compote will keep for 3–4 days.

stewed fruit compote variation

Christmas Stewed Fruit – pour 150ml port into a saucepan, add 75g soft light brown sugar, 2 star anise, 2 cinnamon sticks, 200g stoned prunes, 200g dried figs, stemmed, 200g dried apricots and enough water to cover. Bring to the boil, then simmer for 10 minutes. Add 100g flaked almonds and 150g dried stoned dates. Serve warm or cold.

ONION COMPOTE

A savoury compote and one of the best. Serve with sausages, beef or cheese, use in a quiche or an onion tart, or in sandwiches, spread it in a Welsh rarebit — the possibilities are endless.

Makes one 450g jar

3 tablespoons olive oil

4 large Spanish onions, finely sliced

30g caster sugar

1 rounded teaspoon dried thyme

sea salt and black pepper

1 Put the oil into a frying pan and gently cook the onions until soft. Season well, add the sugar and thyme, then cover the pan and simmer for 30 minutes on a low heat.

2 Store in a sterilised glass jar (see box, page 274). The compote will keep for 1–2 weeks and is delicious served warm or cold.

RUMTOPF

This is such a lovely idea. As fruit comes into season, you add it to the jar, so you have gorgeous soft, alcohol-drenched fruit ready for Christmas. Do be aware, though, that it is very alcoholic indeed. You can buy special rumtopf pots, but a glass preserving jar works just as well — be sure to sterilise it before use (see box, page 274).

Makes 1 large pot

summer and autumn fruit, e.g. strawberries, raspberries, blackcurrants, redcurrants, blackberries, plums, pears, etc.

caster sugar

dark rum

1 Add the fruit to your rumtopf or preserving jar as it comes into season. This usually means starting with the first fruits of the season, like strawberries and raspberries, then continuing to add new fruit as they come into season, finishing with blackberries and plums. Make sure you wash your fruit and dry it on a cloth. You need to hull strawberries, remove any stalks and stone or core and slice large fruit like plums and pears.

2 The classic way of making rumtopf is to layer the fruit with half its weight in sugar in a large jar, and cover it with rum. The layers can be added to as new fruit comes into season. Be sure to cover the pot with a lid so that the rum does not evaporate.